Beautiful One,

I Am with You

Trust and Believe

LaDawn Knicely

This book is dedicated to Jesus Christ, my Lord and Savior, who saw me at my worst, carried me through my darkest nights, and stayed with me through it all, loving me right where I was at. It is only because of Jesus Christ that I am still alive, and that inspired me to write this book from my daily journal entries about wrestling with the flesh against the Spirit. I thank my Lord each and every day for not giving up on me and for rescuing me from the pit of despair.

To my daughter, Kendall, and entire family who endured this journey with me even when they did not understand what God was doing in and through me.

To all of my prayer-warrior partners, sisters and brothers in Christ who encouraged me along the way. You know who you are.

I am so grateful and humbled by what Jesus has done for me. I can't contain this gift, so that is why I am being obedient to God's leading by being a vessel, vulnerable and transparent, about my personal journey. It is all for God's glory to be revealed. God is always faithful.

I n the midst of life, things can happen and change in an instant. I had a life-shattering experience that I did not see coming that was certainly not a part of my plan. This life-shattering experience nearly cost me my life, when I wanted to end it all by committing suicide to stop the deep pain and despair that I felt as a result of my brokenness, living a double life, and traumatic betrayals. This was not the sole reason for my falling apart, but it was a major contributor that finally broke that could no longer hold all of my past traumatic experiences. I no longer knew who I was. I didn't know what my purpose was. I wondered why such bad things happen. I questioned where God was in all of this.

So I began an inward journey with God, where God would take me to my inner depths that I did not know existed, revealing to me my wounds, hidden and known sin, and dark, shadowy parts of myself that had been holding me captive and in bondage to just being complacent and comfortable in my self-gratifying and selfish behaviors.

God revealed to me through my journaling, dreams, meditations, prayer, expressive arts, and contemplation who I was in Christ and who God intended me to be before I was even conceived in my mother's womb.

It has been one of the most painful journeys or disciplines that I have set out to unfold, but it also has been one of the most rewarding gifts that I have given to myself as God has set me free. Now I hope to lead others to be set free in Christ, operating in my God-given authority of intercession and deliverance. It is all about *becoming*.

With love to each of you, LaDawn P. Knicely, MA, MDiv,
minister, pastoral counselor, resident in counseling, blogger,
and author

BECOMING!

Tears catch me off guard,
Flowing from my deep scars,
For it is written
By His stripes I am healed.
What must I know . . .
About the tears from scars?
It is becoming . . .
Becoming?
Becoming one with Jesus:
Having His thoughts, heart, and compassion,
Feeling His connectedness
With family, friends, strangers, and enemies.
Loving the hurt, sick, oppressed, prisoners, and the spiritu-
ally blind,
Hospitality to the least of these,
Stewardship to the earth and all creatures.
I am evolving through His wounds
That touch my wounds;
This is the treasure
That Jesus came to give all.
Becoming new in Christ
So that I too can give all,
Professing hope, faith, belief, and healing
That surpass worldly living.
It is becoming who God intended me to be,

Giving allegiance to Jesus
As a living testimony
Of His deep love, grace, and mercy
That was shed, shed just for me.
When tears catch me off guard,
I know Jesus' wounds
Just touched my wounds.
The tears from the scars,
It is *becoming!*

Devotional Engagement

These devotionals came directly from my daily journal entries as I wrote, prayed, meditated, did dream associations, and reflected on my life-shattering experience. God often spoke back to me words of comfort, affirmation, candid truth, and purpose of why it was necessary for me to go through this transformation.

My hope is that each day as you read the devotional, you will take the time to open the Bible and engage with each Scripture verse that spoke to me at that time. As you read the scripture, I would encourage you to read verses prior and after the recommended scripture. As you do this, keep your personal journal beside you in order to write your personal reflections of what God is wanting you to know or what God's invitation may be for you. This spiritual discipline will open a space within you and expand your capacity to hear God's voice beyond your flesh hearing. This practice will take you deeper to an intimate relationship with God, *becoming* who He intended you to be and do.

May His will be done in your transforming work through Jesus Christ, our Lord and Savior. Amen.

January 1

Beautiful One,

I know you are exhausted and burned out with your normal way of being. I know you are wondering that there must be more purpose and meaning in your life. I know you are questioning your current path and if you are in My perfect will. Continue to seek Me and draw nearer to Me. I will put you on the right path that I intended for you before you were even born. Your childhood circumstances and personal choices took you off the narrow path that I prepared for you. Don't be fearful or anxious, though, because those experiences are going to be used to heal you and make you stronger. I am going to use you so that you can minister to others who may also be experiencing similar trials or hurts. You are going to be the light that sends forth My truth in order to bring others closer to Me. It is going to be an intralife transformational journey for you. As long as you keep focusing on Me, I will reveal Myself in ways that you have never experienced. It will be exhilarating, but it will also take lots of focus and discipline. Part of that discipline is to journal every day about our intimate experience together. Remember, I am with you—Immanuel. Don't question or defend My decisions for you. Settle in and do each absurd thing that surfaces. I have a vision that is too great for you to handle right now. Let Me show you the way in My perfect timing. You just need to trust and believe in Me.

Jeremiah 29:11; Romans 12:2; Philippians 4:6–9; James 4:8

Beautiful One,

You have had your share of failures, temptations, abuses, family circumstances, struggles, and trials. I know this seems to be the lowest point ever in your life. I know you question your self-worth and who you are. It all seems like you have been walking through a fog and have been basically going through the motions, putting on a false persona that you have it all together while on the inside you are weeping and dying. It pains Me that you are carrying this alone and not allowing Me to lift this burden from you. It hurts Me that you have lost your enthusiasm and passion for life. Continue to seek Me with prayer, surround yourself with other Spirit-filled friends, and just keep thanking Me in all of your circumstances even though you don't understand them right now. I have already orchestrated your outcome. I have conquered the worldly ways. In everything, pray. Find space to meditate and be with Me throughout the day. I want to draw nearer to you, Beautiful One.

Isaiah 41:10; 43:19; Hebrews 10:22; James 4:8

January 3

Beautiful One,

I am noticing something in you that is new for you. You are starting to see people in a more compassionate and loving way. Your heart has become tender and aches for others who are experiencing loss, desperation, or trials. As you draw nearer to Me, you will mature more and more in My image. Your faith is increasing, and you are growing spiritually. I am well pleased with your openness to this transformation. As you continue to grow, seek Me more. Part of this process is your learning to let go of the past, let go of control, and depend on Me and not your own strength, desires, or plans. When you rest in My strength, you will have peace and contentment. Allow Me to move and orchestrate matters on your behalf.

Psalm 62:1–2; John 16:33; 2 Thessalonians 3:16;

Beautiful One,

You have been carrying a lot of baggage, hidden sins, and heavy burdens such as lies, deception, anger, hate, bitterness, unforgiveness, pride, shame, and self-centeredness. These feelings and thoughts have nearly destroyed your soul. Beautiful One, you don't have wide-enough shoulders to carry these alone, nor are you supposed to. When you accepted My Son, Jesus Christ, as your Lord and Savior, all of these burdens were wiped away. Let your guard down; come to Me and lay your sins and burdens at the foot of the cross. This will set you free, and I will give you peace and freedom like you have never experienced before. I want to give you peace here on earth like it is in heaven. Come to Me, Beautiful One.

Psalm 51:2; Matthew 11:28; 55:22; 1 John 5:3

Beautiful One,

You think all these trials and burdens are punishment from Me. I tell you the truth; take delight in these circumstances because they are transforming you from the inside out. I am pressing down on you out of love to shape you and mold you into the person that I intended you to be so that you can share with others My grace, mercy, and love. I am preparing you for something significant. I am with you in everything. Pay attention to your surroundings, and notice My presence through others' words of advice, music, Bible verses, nature, and dreams. I use all of these mediums to guide you back to the narrow path. You are going through an intralife spiritual transformation that is not bad thing, but of necessity. It is a beautiful unfolding.

Romans 5:3; 2 Thessalonians 1:4; 1 Peter 4:13

Beautiful One,

I have you now, and I will protect you. You must let go of control, put the past behind you, and let your old self die. Trust in Me and My plan for your life. I am doing great things in your life that you can't see or understand. From this point on, you will not be the same person. If you allow Me, your life will not be your own anymore. I am guiding your thoughts, feelings, choices, and decisions so that you can be My vessel to fulfill My purposes through you. Open your heart, your ears, your eyes, and your nose and begin to recognize My sweet fragrance that is all-encompassing. If you learn to recognize My presence, you will not be fearful, stressed, or anxious. Stay on this path closest to Me.

Psalm 121:7–8; 138:7; 2 Thessalonians 3:3

Beautiful One,

It has been a while since you have spent quiet time with Me in meditation and prayer. The only reason you reached out today was because you recognized My presence in the midst of chaos. I am so glad that you recognized My protection for you and others because it could have been much, much worse. In the midst of this trial, you sought Me and shared My goodness, protection, and thankfulness that everything was going to be all right. I am proud of you that in this circumstance you recognized the reason and purpose that this happened. Sometimes I have to use these situations as a wake-up call to get your attention and draw you closer to Me.

Psalm 30:11–12; 69:30; 100:4

January 14

Beautiful One,

Today I noticed that you made an important realization. Even though you are experiencing personal hurt and pain, your heart is focusing on others instead of yourself. I am proud of you that you recognize that I want to create unity among your brothers and sisters. I want to bring down the walls of division among race, cultures, and religion. This is just one thing that I am revealing to you that will be part of your greater work for Me in My kingdom. I have chosen you for this because of your loving, kind, and compassionate heart. Allow Me to show you how I will use you to create unity.

Psalm 133; Ephesians 4:3; 1 Peter 3:8

Beautiful One,

Why are you trying to strive and earn My attention, love, and grace? Striving is not of Me. That is from the enemy and your overinflated ego that continues to drive you to the point of exhaustion. You can't earn My grace. You have to completely give up control and surrender to Me. Spend time with this driven and striving part of yourself to see where that comes from. Recognize that part of yourself, and acknowledge where that part of yourself comes from. Once you do, you can learn to strip that part away and create unity within all of the other parts of yourself. This inner work is exhausting, but it is also a gift to you from Me. Simply rest and be still in My presence so that you can get to know Me and your inner divine self more intimately. I want you to know that I am right by your side, and I am holding you in the palm of My hand. Use this time to allow Me to give you rest, peace, and comfort. Once you start practicing this time with Me, you will be glad you did and wonder why it took you so long to get here. Be kind and gracious to yourself, though. It is a process.

Psalm 46:10; Isaiah 45:9–11

Beautiful One,

I am so glad that you paid attention to My gentle nudges today and followed the path directly to where I wanted you to be in My perfect timing. It was no coincidence with the interaction that you had with the man along the highway. You also know that because you felt the Holy Spirit upon you. My presence was so powerful that you were trembling and crying, and you did not understand what was happening to you because you are still being spiritually trained. That is why I have put spiritual brothers and sisters in your path, so that you can reach out to them when you don't understand what is going on within you spiritually. They gave you wise counsel and prayers from Me today. Just think, if you would not have spent time with Me and asked Me to reveal to you what I wanted you to know, you would have missed that the man along the highway was actually My Son, Jesus Christ, that you looked directly into His eyes. My lesson from this is that I want you to learn to pay attention to My gentle nudges and follow where I am directing you. Remember that for everyone you encounter, look to see My Son, Jesus Christ, in their eyes, and stop to take time to be in communion with Me and not be so busy with worldly distractions.

Psalm 16:7; 1 Corinthians 1:9; 2 Corinthians 13:14

Beautiful One,

That was a kind act that you expressed today in surprising your sweet sister in faith. You blessed her so at the right moment when she needed it most. I gave her a message to let you know that you are the King's child, and I have an amazing plan for you. I am going to bless you and keep you, and My face is going to continue to shine upon you each and every day. I love you and so appreciate your willingness to walk in obedience to My plan and will for your life. I am going to continue to amaze you in ways that you never could comprehend from this world. Thank you for opening your heart, eyes, and ears even though you still seem to feel like you are going through the storm. I see and know the scars on your heart. I am going to restore and renew your heart. I am going to use you, child—yes, use you because you are obedient and willing to praise Me in all things. I love your humble heart.

Numbers 6:24–26; Philippians 5:2–8

Beautiful One,

You amaze Me in your desire to attain more knowledge and wisdom from My promised words. I love it that you are working on enhancing all of your relationships with your family, friends, and those who are going to be put in front of you. You are pressing forward to improve your individual self even though you are suffering greatly as you are doing this work. There is a reason and purpose in enduring this suffering. When you endure suffering, it is softening your heart so that you can be compassionate toward yourself and more importantly toward others. This is an important transformational lesson for you at this moment. Be patient and kind with yourself. I delight and will give favor and blessing for each and every tear you have shed. I know it has been many tears. Know that these tears are not for nothing. You have been called for a purpose. As you know, My Son, Jesus Christ, also suffered for you. Therefore, you have an example that you can follow while I am transforming you. Keep trusting and believing in Me, and do not let your heart harden. That is what the enemy would like to happen.

Romans 8:17; 1 Peter 2:18–23; 5:10

Beautiful One,

Meditate on My precepts today of how I want you to live your life. Continue to praise Me repeatedly, as it helps to purify your heart and cause you to grow in faith. My Word will inspire you to live your life fully in My name. Memorize My Word, and it will strengthen you to help you avoid temptation to sin and worldly influences. My Word will be your guide to the narrow path that I have planned for you. My Word will give you freedom and My best for your life if you completely surrender to Me. We will journey together; let Me show you how. You are so worthy and deserving of My love. I can't wait to reveal My orchestrated plan for you that will bring people's hearts to Me and change their lives. I will fill you and equip you with My Spirit, love, wisdom, and knowledge. I am using all of your past failures, successes, pain, suffering, and joy to strengthen you. Do not fear or have doubt in My plans and calling for your life. I am your sovereign God, and you are My humble servant in whom I take delight.

Psalm 119

Beautiful One,

I am noticing your spiritual maturity and devotion to My Word. I will give you an abundance of grace and peace because I see the effort that you are putting forth in studying and meditating on My Word. As you grow in My knowledge and become more Christlike, you become ever more empowered to resist temptation, develop perseverance, gain obedience and discipline, have an unwavering faith, be in My complete will, and share loving-kindness to all that you meet. In all parts of your life, you will gain a self-controlled balance that will give you peace, wellness, and wholeness that can come only from Me, your heavenly Father. As you continue to mature in these qualities, there is an increase in your character that will make you fully productive and effective in all areas of your life to serve Me fully.

Proverbs 28:6; Romans 5:3–5; 1 Peter 1:1–11

January 21

Beautiful One,

You are finally noticing the plans that I am placing on your heart. Now you need to trust and believe in Me to show you how to make them come to fruition. Pay attention to the vision that I give you. I will direct your path, give you the resources, and put the people into your life that you need to make it all come to fruition. Watch Me orchestrate this and make things happen in your life. You will be amazed at how easily it all comes together effortlessly. I will reveal to you that I am in control and making things happen. In all of this, watch Me work in your life. You will gain an understanding of My power and what it means to be in My perfect will. I will help you carry out My plans perfectly.

Psalm 146:8; Habakkuk 2:2; Romans 8:24

Beautiful One,

You are becoming an extraordinarily strong person. I see your determination, and when I place something on your heart, you pursue it wholeheartedly and nothing gets in your way. I see you growing in patience and trust. You are a person with great perseverance who continues to show Me that you press through all of your personal suffering and obstacles. You are becoming a very strong individual who will empower others. I am most impressed with your ability to incorporate a personal spiritual-wellness plan into your life that focuses on your physical, relational, family, spiritual, mental, emotional, and financial well-being. Having balance in all of these areas gives you the enlightenment and wholeness that you have desired for many years. Stay invigorated with this plan, and I will take care of the rest in your life. This plan that you follow will also be shared by you with others that I place in your path.

Matthew 5:6; 1 Corinthians 6:19; 3 John 1:2

Beautiful One,

You seem down and depressed. I have noticed that you are sleeping a lot and pulling away from Me. I see your broken heart; I notice your anger toward Me, and even though you don't speak it, I know your dissatisfied thoughts of where you are right now. You think that I am not near you, but I am. You again are trying to fix or control things by coming up with answers and solutions. Right now, none of this makes sense to you. I do hear your prayers and I do know your heart, but you are not ready for the truth yet. At this point, you are not ready to handle what is coming next. Take this time to lean in closer to Me, knowing that I have your best interests at heart for you, My beloved child.

2 Samuel 22:31; Psalm 18:30; Isaiah 55:8

Beautiful One,

You are gaining clarity and understanding with the ability to hear Me speak into you. I want to confirm for you that you have heard correctly and you are supposed to:
1. Let go of control.
2. *Trust* and *Believe* Me.
3. I am your Beloved and Husband.
4. Seek only Me at all times.
5. Do not fear.
6. Thank Me in all your circumstances.
7. Don't seek or strive for approval from others.
8. Stop clinging to old ways.
9. Accept and be content with each new day that I give you.
10. Reach for My hand instead of temporary worldly pleasures.

Psalm 115:3; Proverbs 3:5–6; Zechariah 4:6

Beautiful One,

I give a peace that most do not understand. You are starting to comprehend it and fully embrace it in your own life. The peace that I want to fill the earth with is a peace that brings unity with one another, a peace that creates wellness and wholeness. This means we share with our brothers and sisters the breaking of bread, food, shelter, education, clean water, medical care, loving-kindness, and compassion. If everyone has access to these things, they can experience self-worth, dignity, and whole being. Beautiful One, there is a ministry that is unfolding to make this possible. I will send others to you so that you can minister to them in this capacity so that they may know and experience My peace fully. We have much work to do, but just simply rest, knowing I have prepared the way and resources. Trust and believe by continuing to walk the steps that I have directed for you. You are on the right path.

Psalm 18:32–36; John 16:33; Colossians 3:15

January 26

Beautiful One,

I see your aching heart, the feeling of rejection, thinking you have been abandoned and are all alone in this. Don't pay attention to the negative and cold feelings that you are receiving from others. I see your struggles and your suicidal thoughts. You are so much greater than those feelings of low self-worth and hopelessness. The enemy wants you to believe those lies. The reason he wants you to believe those lies is that he knows you continue to walk on My path that I have directed for you. I know sometimes you feel like you are just walking through the motions, but I do see your effort, and you are making progress. Know that you are on the right path, My beautiful child.

Psalm 39:7; Jeremiah 29:11–13; Romans 12:12

January 27

Beautiful One,

Do not be angry or bitter at your trials and adversity. Be sure to count it all joy for blessings are being cultivated and multiplied at this place. You do not perceive it yet, but it all truly has meaning and purpose that you will come to understand. For when you are weak and needy, My grace is all sufficient and abounding in love. Cast out your fears and anxious thoughts for they are not My ways. I am with you in the midst of your storm, and I will see you through it.

Psalm 34:5; 2 Corinthians 12; James 1:2-3; 1 Peter 5:10

January 28

Beautiful One,

Your difficulties and circumstances do not define who you are. Use this time to strengthen your faith, and I will bless you with favor. Continue to press forward through the storms keeping your focus upon Me. Acknowledge Me in all things, and I will surely direct your path in the way that you should go. I know you have felt many times like giving up and questioning whether I am really with you. I have never promised to make the journey easy, but I can promise you that you will be glad you stayed on it and finished the race. Keep pressing forward. We are only beginning.

Exodus 15:2; Psalm 18:32–34; Proverbs 3:6

January 29

Beautiful One,

You are starting to recognize your hidden potential and gifts that I have impregnated within you. This is the start of a new beginning for you to carry out My plan. As part of your spiritual transformation, I am leading you to unite relationships in My name regardless of religious background, race, and culture. Allow Me to show you how to cultivate relationships with a loving, peaceful nurturance that will build bridges for forgiveness and healing among individuals, cultures, and communities.

Galatians 6:2; Philippians 2:3–16; Hebrews 10:24–25

Beautiful One,

You continue to open your heart to Me, which allows Me to fill you with inner peace, wellness, and wholeness. I know your needs and will meet your needs. Continue to focus on Me, trust in Me, and give Me your loyalty, and I will continue to work out the personal issues, burdens, and relationships in your life. Only I can change these things, but only you can make a choice and decision to rely upon Me. Continue to be obedient, and I will make your path clear so that you do not doubt My plan for you. Be spiritually strong in My name, and I will take care of everything else. Recognize that you are not strong enough, but I am. Rebuke the enemy continually because he is trying to get a foothold in you in any way that he can. Pray the Ephesians prayer for protection for you and your family. I am equipping and empowering you to minister to others. Remember that the victory is already won in the name of My Son, Jesus Christ.

2 Samuel 22:3–4; Psalm 5:11 ; Ephesians 6:10–18

January 31

Beautiful One,

You are victorious in all things in My name. Remember that in all things, when you acknowledge Me, I direct your path. Stay close to Me, and I will not let you miss the next thing. I see your enthusiasm in getting to know Me more intimately. It delights Me to see your spirit and faith growing, especially when you are willingly pursuing Me instead of Me seeking you out.

Proverbs 3:6; Romans 8:37; 1 Corinthians 15:57

Beautiful One,

I know you still struggle with letting go of the past. You allowed your past relationships, careers, and possessions to come before Me. That is a form of idolatry that had to be stripped away from you. I know that is painful to hear and accept, especially when you had your own plans and desires that I intervened with. You don't understand right now, but you will one day thank Me. I have noticed everything that you are doing in My name by fasting, crying, praying, and serving in order to receive answered prayers. You have given Me an ultimatum, and that is not how I work. When you pray and fast, you must confess your sins, and then I will give you a new, pure, and renewed heart. That is how you receive My grace and mercy that is offered to you.

Proverbs 16:3; Matthew 6:19–21, 33

Beautiful One,

I see all of your weaknesses and lack of patience. During this time, I am strengthening you, but I need you to be content with where I have you right now. You need to trust and believe Me and be assured that there is hope in this situation. I am working in all areas of your life to renew you and purify your heart. You are letting the enemy control your thoughts and emotions. When you allow this, it enrages you with anxious and fearful thoughts, where you say and do things you regret later. Rebuke the enemy and focus on Me. I can calm your thoughts and emotions if you come to Me. I want to be your everything.

Psalm 55:22; Matthew 11:28; 1 Peter 5:7

February 3

Beautiful One,

Now that I have captured all of your heart, I am commanding you to go, go, go with each and every person that you encounter and introduce them to Me. Take each and every opportunity to be in relationship with others and to love them just as I love you. No matter where they are, what they have done, just love them. Loving them will open their hearts to Me by your example of accepting and not judging them. When you accept them and care for them in this way, they feel worthy and deserving of My love. I want to capture each and every soul. Know that I have chosen you to do great things in My name. Don't question why I have chosen you. I am not done with you yet. We have only begun, My victorious child.

Matthew 5:14–16; Matthew 25:21; Titus 2:7

Beautiful One,

   I know you have been reflecting on My choice to choose you to do My work. It is true that I have chosen you. I choose the ordinary and the foolish ones. Keep doing every absurd or foolish thing that I put before you to bring others to Me. Just as I have turned you inside out and upside down, I am also going to turn this world upside down and inside out. I will do whatever is necessary in order to get everyone to confess My Son, the Lord Jesus Christ, as Savior. There is a movement of My Holy Spirit going across this nation. Just know that I am right beside you all the way, every day. I have provided a full body of armor of protection around you. Continue to trust, obey, believe, and have steadfast faith. Your battles have been won.

   Isaiah 42:1; 1 Corinthians 1:27; Colossians 3:12–17

February 5

Beautiful One,

I notice your obedience and willingness to reach out and touch others in need. Your words of encouragement and small token gifts make others feel and know My presence. They experience My love and feel special by your small acts of kindness. You are beginning to accept and know that I have in fact chosen you to ministry. You are going to make a significant impact and difference in people's lives. Draw nearer to Me, and I will reveal to you how powerful I am. You are so precious in My sight.

Luke 6:38; Galatians 5:22–23; Ephesians 4:32

February 6

Beautiful One,

I am pleased with your training and discipline with the spiritual, emotional, and mental growth you have shown. It is during this time that I continue to search your heart and count your tears. I know at times you pull away from Me and rebel against where I currently have you. You seem to be just going through the motions, but that is okay. I recognize your efforts. I know that you feel like the weight of the world is pressing down on you. That is the way it feels when you try to do everything in your strength. Give it to Me. My shoulders are wide, and I want to make your burdens light.

Psalm 16:8; 56:3–4; 2 Corinthians 4:17

Beautiful One,

I see your desperate and distraught ways. I don't think I have ever seen you in so much pain to the point of feeling sick. Beautiful One, know that there is nothing in this world that is worth ending or harming your own life. This is the evil work of the enemy that is making you feel and react in this way. Come to Me and lay your head on My chest. I will comfort you and dry your tears. I am so proud of you for finding meaning and purpose in your life to live for Me and others. Pay attention to the nineteen blessings that will be coming your way. Be sure to document them in your journal as reminders of My work and promises.

Job 5:11; Psalm 55:22; Revelation 21:4

Beautiful One,

You still have not submitted or let go of control. Now you are at a place where finances are tight, business is down, your vehicle has broken down, your basement foundation wall has caved in, and you feel as though you are going to collapse. I did not want it to come to this, but this is what it has taken to get you to the point to ask the right question. You have continually been asking Me *why* instead of *what*. This is what I have been waiting for—for you to ask Me, "What is it that You want me to learn from all of this? What is it that I need to improve or change? What is it that I need to let go of and give total surrender to You?" This is a time of My molding and refining you to get you on the path that I have directed for you. Instead of complaining, lashing out, and turning away from Me, simply humble yourself in My presence so that I can reveal to you the greater plan for your life. Thank you for giving Me your full, undivided attention. Now I can reveal more to you.

1 Samuel 15:23; Isaiah 45:9; Romans 13:2

February 9

Beautiful One,

Give in to My refining process so that I can make you
My perfect gem. This process will help you gain My perfect
knowledge, truth, and wisdom so that you will be able to teach and
help others with where you have been. I know how exhausting and
overwhelming this process has been. Just remember that I never
give you more than you can handle. I have been patiently waiting
for you to get to this point.

Psalm 51:6; Proverbs 2:6; 8:11–12

Beautiful One,

Be careful what you ask for. You have been asking, "Where are You? Why won't You answer me? Why won't You give me a sign or vision?" Well, this evening was the perfect storm to reveal Myself. You were not in danger, but I wanted to show you My strength and power and how I can reveal Myself in mysterious ways. Even though the storm was not close, it was a perfect way for Me to reveal Myself through a loud clap of thunder and a flashing bolt of lightning that flashed in your face. Yes, you felt Me in that moment. It was My warmth that you felt on your face and My light that blinded your eyes. I wanted to get your attention by being firm, but also sent you a loving reminder that I do hear you. My message is to surrender to Me and to be still.

Job 37:2–12; Psalm 29:3

February 11

Beautiful One,

Yes, I use everything in My power to communicate to you,
even thunder and lightning. It was My way to quicken you and
show you My power and presence. Keep your eyes and focus on
Me. Pay attention to even the smallest synchronicity that I put
before you. It is probably a message that I have for you, but you
need to be still and in My presence to receive it. Be careful and
cautious because the enemy will try to give you false messages.
That is why it is so important to stay near Me and know the
ways in which I communicate with you. When you feel unsafe
or threatened, just proclaim and keep repeating, "The Lord is my
Savior, the Lord is my Savior, the Lord is my Savior." I am your
protector, provider, rescuer, lover, keeper, and Savior.

Psalm 91

February 12

Beautiful One,

It was no accident that your long-time friend reached out and contacted you. It is My way of showing you that I am in control and at work in your life, orchestrating your divine steps. It was no accident that your friend told you that I am going to use all of the previous skills you have acquired for use in ministry. Your friend also told you that you are perfect for My ministry because of your sensitive and kind way of being. She said that My plans are significant for you. It's been over twenty-plus years since you both have seen each other. How else do you think she would have known to contact you and share this message with you? It is another example of how I use others to direct your steps and give you affirmation along the way.

Proverbs 11:14; 13:20; 19:20; 24:5

February 13

Beautiful One,

Self-doubt is not of Me. That is condemnation from the enemy. Don't let the enemy begin to plant that seed of deceit. When I want to convict or reveal something to you, I will let you know specifically what it is. In your faith, I need you to be hot and close to Me in everything. *If you are lukewarm, you are inadequate, and I will spit you out.* Don't be independent or self-sufficient because you will be ineffective. Depend fully on Me, giving Me glory in all your circumstances and situations. Don't be spiritually blind. Ask Me in all things for the truth and understanding of what I want you to know through this day and each and every day. I operate only in truth and will give you only the truth.

John 17:17; Romans 8:1; Revelation 3:16

February 14

Beautiful One,

I know, feel, and have examined your heart. Your heart is heavy, full of doubts and fears. Beautiful One, open your heart to Me and let Me in. I want to show you My face. I want you to hear My voice. I want to reveal to you My plan for your life. I want you to be at peace and stress free. I want to give you what you are so desiring and deserving of. I desire a dependent relationship with you. Let Me show you how to get there. Do not believe the lies of the enemy, condemning you and making you feel not loved, imperfect, and not worthy to be loved. Those are lies! I will never condemn you, even when you mess up. I will always love you, no matter what. I will always love you, despite your imperfect ways. I want to come down and write a new plan and song in your heart that no one can ever take away from you and that will replace the existing scars. I love you so dearly, Beautiful One, and I no longer want you to feel so empty. Open your heart and continually invite Me in. I am here with you.

1 Kings 8:61; Ephesians 1:18; Hebrews 10:22

February 15

Beautiful One

I am a loving and compassionate God who so desires for us to be in an intimate relationship with each other so that you can share this love with others that you meet. To become spiritually mature, I need you to let go, give up your independence, depend only on Me, trust in Me wholeheartedly, and walk peacefully one step at a time. When the time is right, I will reveal to you what My plan is for your life. Just be content during this time, and I will give you the balance, wellness, and wholeness that you so desire. I am making you Spirit-filled during this time so that I can use you to empower others so that they too will know they are loved and worthy. I want others to know Me intimately and also want to reveal My plan for them by shining My face upon them. You will be a witness to My work in others.

Psalm 86:15; 103:8; 145:8

February 16

Beautiful One,

I am so glad you had your first experience with soaking prayer. It is just another way that I can reveal My power by using others who do not know you or your circumstances to speak My words over you. Yes, this is a time of changing seasons for you—a new dawn, if you like, as your name indicates. All of your challenges and tough circumstances are getting ready to change. It is as if you are preparing your garden to plant seeds in the spring so that they can get ready to sprout. Even though you don't see it or feel it, you too are getting ready to spiritually grow and sprout in more ways than you can imagine. You are at that door again, afraid to open it. You need to have courage so you can go through the door. I know your thoughts and prayers. I do hear them, and progress is being made even though you may not physically see it. Your heart is full of anxiousness, but you must be patient with where you are. Small steps are being made. I know your heart and what you are asking for.

Isaiah 58:8; Luke 8

February 17

Beautiful One,

You have such a gift of being able to see the heart and spirit in others. With this gift, you are going to be able to minister to people in profound ways. Ask Me to continue to strengthen you, lead you, and quicken you. I will give you courage, boldness, and peace within your spirit so that you will know exactly how to use this gift. In order to keep within this gift, you must continue to stay within Me. Apart from Me, you will be ineffective, and this gift will be temporal and unstable. I am equipping you to be an instrument to help others who come to you. Whoever wants to save his life will lose it, but whoever loses his life for Me will find it. Others who know you or come to you may not understand your new way of being. Be strong and steadfast, and don't give in to their ways. Continue on this path, and you will be like a stone that is dropped into a pond that will create a ripple effect changing the lives of others around you. It will not be an easy process, so praise Me in everything, and do not trust mortal men.

Psalm 146; Matthew 16:25

Beautiful One,

I have a strong message for you. Everyone that you meet, whether believers or not, everyone needs to be validated; they need to know that they are worthy to be loved and that they already have Me who loves them dearly, and I want to get close to them. Others that you meet are going to be on different paths and may or may not know Me. But I tell you the truth, we are to *love all—all* our neighbors—whether they are sinners, friends, church family, outsiders, family, or those from different faiths and cultures. You are called to reach out and *love all* and share My message of salvation. Make use of each and every opportunity. Be gracious when you do this, and always respect and seek to understand others so that they will be open to receive My promises and truth that you are going to share with them.

Psalm 43:3; Colossians 4:2–6

Beautiful One,

I know that another friend of yours told you today that you are going to be in ministry. I saw your tears. I know these are happy tears, but also tears of feeling unworthy of this calling and the uncertainty that it brings. Accept My calling for you, and continue to do each and every thing that I put on your path. I know this is taking you out of your comfort zone, but I applaud you for doing each and every thing that I put before you. Stepping out in faith delights Me greatly. It shows Me that you are relying more and more on Me. Just know that if you do stumble, I am there to hold you up. I will not let you fail and want to give to you abundantly.

Ephesians 2:1–10; 6:7; 2 Timothy 1:9

Beautiful One,

I am so excited that you have been obedient and have accepted the path that I have for you. It thrills Me to see your enthusiasm and joy. Yes, I know you still are in disbelief for the path that I have prepared for you. As I have told you, just keep doing the next thing where I lead you. As you follow this way, I will make the path clear, and all of the circumstances in your life will fall into place effortlessly. We are going to be on an amazing journey together, and you are going to watch Me unfold miraculous events in your life. Keep close to Me, and I will lead you each step of the way. You will have a lot to juggle, but it can be done in My strength and My strength alone. Share with others the strength, truth, and promises that I have bestowed upon you in your life. You will be a living example of what I can do in others' lives too if they simply surrender by letting go and let Me.

Proverbs 4:25–27; Ephesians 5:1–21; Titus 2:7

February 21

Beautiful One,

You are growing in empathy, compassion, and loving kindness for others with the ability to feel and know their pain and burdens. This can be overwhelming at times. I want you to know that this is not for you to carry, but for you to stop and have intercessory prayer for those whom your path crosses. You do not have to do this in their presence, but you can stop where you are and pray for them unknowingly. Just pray with whatever comes to mind in spirit or tongues. When you do this, you are also keenly aware that My Holy Spirit is upon you because you feel My warmth and tremble uncontrollably. It pleases Me that you are practicing new spiritual experiences. As you experience My work, visualize the shackles and chains falling away from your wrists and ankles. Thank Me for prying them away from your grip, releasing you from pain, heavy burdens, and sin. Experience this wonderful feeling because I have set you free. I am equipping you to set others free too.

John 8:32; Galatians 5:1

Beautiful One,

When I place something on your heart, follow through with it no matter how busy you are. React and put your faith into action no matter how busy your schedule is, what little time you have, or how limited your resources may be. When I place something on your heart, I will give you abundant time, relationships, and resources. I want you to trust Me enough to press forward with the idea so that I can show you My hand and glory in the process to make it come to fruition. It has to be done in My power and not yours. Be My hands and feet by allowing Me to use you. Remember that when the plan comes from Me, I have already prepared the way and have taken care of each and every detail. Thank you for continuing to be close to Me. I love unfolding surprises before your eyes. I delight in your amazement and awe of My work. I can't wait to reveal to you what is next.

Psalm 37:4–6; Titus 1:16; James 2:17

Beautiful One,

I am pleased that you want to show your true commitment to Me by serving, giving, and fasting. Oftentimes on your spiritual journey you can forget the importance of fasting. It takes discipline and obedience to fast and be in My perfect will. When you are in complete obedience to Me, I can reveal things to you that you would have otherwise missed. Watch for your special blessings and favors during this time. Relax in knowing that you are right where you are supposed to be, and accept My peace that I give you. I have seen and heard your preconceived ideas and goals, but trust Me that as you let go of control, I can reveal My plans more fully to you each day as you relinquish your wishes and desires. It is a journey with Me each day. Enjoy the journey because that is as important as the destination that I have planned for you. I know your needs and have prepared and will provide.

Ecclesiastes 4:12; John 14:15; Revelation 14:12

Beautiful One,

I am so pleased that you have allowed Me to work in your life. I have noticed that you have opened your heart, eyes, and ears to My presence. It is so important to know My voice and My presence so that you can receive all that I have for you to do in My name here on earth to bring people to Me. As you become spiritually strong, more will come to you in the way of visions, ideas, and resources. As you have noticed, I have already made ways possible for you that never were a part of your plan. This is an exciting time in your life, a new chapter and new journey, none like you have ever experienced before. Even though your experiences are new, pay attention to the calm and peace that is surrounding you. I know this is a new feeling and way of being for you. I see your excitement for this opportunity. I see your willingness to follow. I see you take this seriously and that you want to be in My complete will. I have chosen you to impact and restore the lives of people that I place in your path. Thank you for your altruistic spirit and service to Me and My kingdom.

Genesis 3:8; Jeremiah 29:12–13; John 10:27

February 25

Beautiful One,

Your prayer today touched Me. You have completely surrendered your life to Me. You have given up control. You stated that your life is not your own, and you thanked Me for rescuing you from the path of soul destruction. I know you still have strong emotions and experience hurt, pain, desires, and burdens. This is what impresses Me the most. Despite your deepest hurts, pain, desires, and burdens, you have faithfully committed your life totally to Me. This is when I can do the greatest work in your life. Your faith is so strong, and I have promised you that I have plans to prosper you and not harm you. I am going to show you My glory. I assure you, this is only the beginning of great things to come your way.

Jeremiah 29:11; Acts 20:24

Beautiful One,

I assure you that in all of your pain, I am with you. Even though you don't see or feel the healing, I am working in all areas of your life. This time is for you to solely rely on Me. Open your eyes, ears, and heart. Once you open up to Me, I can speak into you and give you visions. I want to give you the peace, joy, hope, and love that I have promised to those who love Me. I want to offer you these gifts. I want to fully live in you and through you so that you can have the life that I intended you to live. I will show you the way. I have already anointed you for this time and purpose. Just keep saying that you trust and believe in Me. Trust and believe! In My perfect timing, you will see everything new. Have faith and believe that your prayers will be answered. I delight in you and just ask that you be patient and continue to praise Me through your heartache.

Psalm 104:33–34; Micah 2:13; John 6:47

February 27

Beautiful One,

Today should be a joyous day for you; however, I see your
heavy heart and the pain you are carrying. I see and hear your
confusion of not knowing what to do or how to make all the pain
and racing thoughts subside. I will take control of all of this if you
will relinquish your control. I give you free will to make choices
and decisions, so you must make a choice to give up control. Once
you give up control, I can intervene and carry this for you. I see
your desperation and hear your thoughts that you feel like you are
losing it. You question My love, purpose, and plan for you. That is
the enemy confusing you, and you are missing My gentle whispers
to you. Keep pressing forward with pursuing Me, wanting to be
more intimate with Me, and you can receive all of your gifts of the
Spirit. I will use you if you allow Me to use you.

1 Corinthians 14:33; 2 Timothy 2:7; 1 John 4:1

Beautiful One,

Part of giving up control is also stopping to try to "fix" everything for everyone. In your control and need to fix everything, you or no one else would need Me. This has been ingrained in you from an early age, so I know this will be one of the hardest disciplines that will need to be stripped from you. This overbearing driven part of you exhausts you, and you become unproductive and are always pulled in different directions. You become overwhelmed. Be still and meditate in My presence to see what I reveal to you. You have already come so far and persevered through so many trials. Now I need you to trust and rest in My presence because I have already prepared the way for you. Now I want you to delight in the simple joys that I bring your way. Take delight in Me, your family, your work, your studies, your relationships, and daily activities. More importantly, take delight in where I have you right now. It is no mistake that you are right where you need to be. I am transforming you and guiding you on the lighted path that I have prepared for you. Delight in being still and quiet in My presence.

Psalm 61:2; 142:3; John 14:1

Beautiful One,

As you are coming nearer to Me, you are starting to see parts of yourself that your overbearing ego made you into. It is good to recognize these parts of fear, shame, guilt, control, pride, bitterness, selfishness, sin, and ambition. These parts do not have to control you, nor do they represent who you truly are. This is part of the transformational process to recognize these dying, wilting parts in this season. This is why your life has been filled with chaos, unhappiness, brokenness, and unfulfilling desires. This is why you feel completely burned out and have nothing left to give. The good news is that a new season is being birthed. It won't be easy, but if you obediently come to Me in all things, I will reveal to you the purpose and will for your life. On this journey, I will shower you with My joy, peace, and fulfillment that this world can't give you. I am inviting you to allow My Spirit to move in your midst so that so you can experience My grace in a deeply profound way.

Ezra 9:7; Psalm 37:5–6; 8:3–4; 2 Timothy 3:6

Beautiful One,

I have seen you seek Me passionately with your prayers and giving. You don't always hear from Me because I want you to seek Me more. This seeking is what has gotten you to this point of denying yourself and fasting. My followers utilize prayer, giving and service, but oftentimes forget about the importance of fasting. Fasting takes your relationship to a deeper intimacy. During this time of fasting, be sure to journal and listen for My voice. I know it is a constant struggle and conflict with you. I have heard your cries and have noticed your rebellion against My will and purpose for your life. It is okay to communicate your anger and to question why I have allowed things to unfold the way they have. I value your bringing all of your concerns to Me. I see your frustration and exhaustion. You are now at a place of surrender and will allow Me to do My work in you and through you. This is not for you to figure out. I simply want you to obey Me and trust in My plan for you, and I will unfold it effortlessly if you just let Me show you how.

Nehemiah 1:4; Ecclesiastes 4:12;

March 3

Beautiful One,

You still question and demand answered prayers. You question whether I am even listening to your prayers and wondering if I am with you. You should be cautious what you ask for. I have been revealing things to you, but you have not noticed them because you are so self-absorbed with your personal wants and desires. That is why I showed up in the form of thunder and a lightning bolt directly in your face. There was no storm around or near you, so that is what I thought would get your attention. The lightning that flashed in front of your face was not to harm you, but to let you know that I am near you and hear you. The blinding flash and heat that you felt on your face was the sound of thunder that is My glorious voice. You can't even imagine the greatness of My strength, but you did get to experience a fraction of My power. You would not have been able to experience the fullness of My power. I am glad that you felt Me to the point of experiencing fear and trembling, but yet you had peace, knowing that I did this only to get your attention, not to harm you. I have nothing but love, grace, and mercy for you. I want to reveal your life purpose and new way of being so that you can selflessly serve others.

Numbers 22:24–27; Job 37:4–5; Matthew 6:34

Beautiful One,

This process of shedding old ways and habits I know seems unending and tireless. I see the great strides and progress that you are making. You are growing spiritually in so many ways with your emotions, physical well-being, relational well-being, and wisdom. Growing in all of these areas will eventually lead you to a feeling of wellness, peace, and wholeness, which you have so desired. You are beginning to understand that this process is leading you into ministry in some capacity. Just trust in Me and know that this process is temporary. When the timing is right, I will give you the vision to open the next door when you are ready. I hold that key to open the next door. You are near to having the key placed in the door to unlock the next step. In the meantime, you must just keep repeating, "I shall believe" and mean it.

Romans 12:1–2; Ephesians 4:22–24; 1 John 2:15–17

Beautiful One,

I have noticed that you have not been able to find that personal space and time to be with Me. Your heart feels so restricted and wrapped up in thousands of strands of wire. This wire is from the past and is so tight. The wire represents so many past hurts, failures, and trials. You feel like no one notices, appreciates, or cares about you. You feel depleted and burned out. I notice the gray-and-black cloud that surrounds your heart. All of your responsibilities are weighing you down to the point you feel overwhelmed. Give this all to Me. I have promised not to give you more than you can handle. I have promised that as you pass through the waters, I will be there with you, and when you pass through the rivers, they will not sweep over you. When you walk through the fire, you will not be burned; the flames will not set you ablaze. I am the Lord your God, the Holy One of Israel, your Savior. I will be there with you as you start to pull away each tightly wrapped strand of wire. I am yearning for you to have that space to be in communion with Me. I know this is a painful and emotional process because it goes so deep. You never realized how deep it is and how present it is in your everyday life, affecting you and others in your relationships. I am with you during this process, so fear not. Unwrap those buried strands of wire. You are so precious to Me, and I love you.

Isaiah 43:2–5

Beautiful One,

I am so thankful you were able to find some time to be with Me and near Me. As you looked out at the beauty of the majestic mountains at the overlook, I felt your loving appreciation for My beauty and the warmth of your heart as you meditated on My words. It pleased Me that you could relax on the ground and receive my comforting thoughts for you:

The sun is warm, like My comforting
Arms around you.
The wind is like My breath and
Spirit all around you.
The views are majestic, just like
My awesome power.

I hope you realize that this was as surreal of a moment for Me as it was for you. This time that we spend together is an invigorating feeling. Just as I created the beautiful landscape, I beautifully created you too. Don't ever forget that. You are My beautiful creation in whom I take delight. Thank you for spending your time meditating with Me, surrounded by My creation.

Psalm 139

Beautiful One,

As you grow and mature spiritually, so will others close to you grow. I know you were not expecting this, and you were in disbelief that I could give such words to your daughter. This is how I work and like to show you My work and glory. Not only am I making your heart tender during this process, but I am also creating a more compassionate and loving place within others nearest to you. This is what I spoke into your daughter today:

Tears are nothing to fear; I am already here. I will make your path lighted, and you will have nothing to fear. I am putting My arms around you just like a shield of love and peace. I will always be there for you. I might not answer your prayers the night you say them, but I will make them happen. I am your Savior and the light in your heart. I love to hear you sing, pray, and praise Me. I am forever.

Deuteronomy 31:8; Psalm 27:1; Isaiah 35:4

Beautiful One,

As you reflect on where you have been and where you are headed, you are recognizing the things that you need to let go of. You need to let go of control, striving, fear, success, ambition, and yes, yourself. As you let go of these things, you will gain wisdom, knowledge, more personal space, time for meditation, balance, spiritual mystery, energy, and My plan unfolding for you. As you gain this new way of being, you will experience success that is different from what you have known in the past. Success is having a balance in your life that is so much greater than you that it can't be measured or held on to. Your success will be displayed by your altruistic, selfless service that will be shared with others and that will create a ripple effect in them that will allow them to know Me more. As they begin to know Me more, there will be a cycle and balance of mental, relational, physical, emotional, and spiritual wellness. This is the process of My hollowing you out of the old ways and habits so that My light can flow freely through you and into others. There is no measure that can determine what success may look like. I can only promise you that there will be abundance.

Isaiah 43:18–19; Luke 9:62; Philippians 3:12–14

Beautiful One,

As you are journeying with Me, you are beginning to recognize the gifts that I have equipped you with. It is important to know and utilize these gifts that I have given you. My hope is that as you name these gifts, you can begin to realize that they are necessary and are what drives your passion and desires for others and the community. As your creator, I bestow wisdom upon you to work for others on social-justice issues, human rights, and peace. That is why I have given you the gift of hospitality and mercy. You are natural at making others feel at ease and welcome no matter their background, faith, or past. You show mercy to all and accept them where they are in life. Just like My Son, Jesus Christ, you are committed to loving relationships. Your gifts of apostle, counseling, and missionary will serve you well as you are working and walking with others who are going through troubled and painful times. My Holy Spirit gives you supernatural power and faith like no other. As you are working with individuals, your faith and intercessory prayer will serve them and you well. Continue to grow in these gifts, and watch Me work wonders in your life. You are beginning to understand that success is utilizing all of these gifts and talents to the best of your ability, enhancing others' lives. For that, I am well pleased with you.

Romans 12:6–8; 1 Corinthians 12

March 10

Beautiful One,

It was no accident that today you experienced a paranormal event. The explosion and shattering of the glass that burst with a loud explosion and blew thousands of pieces of glass all over you and the room for twenty-five feet was symbolic of Me finally shattering your egotistical world as you knew it. I saw your disbelief, but also your peace of knowing that this was a message from Me that this was the last phase of shattering your life and old ways. You accepted this process well by joyfully picking up all the pieces of glass instead of showing hostility and anger. I am glad you recognized that this is the beginning of a new phase where you will, one by one, pick up the pieces, but I will be in control of placing them back into the beautiful places where they belong. Listen and follow Me obediently so that you are aware of where each place is to be lovingly placed. I can't wait to reveal to you what My final masterpiece in you will look like. You will be in awe.

Ephesians 2:10

Beautiful One,

I enjoy you singing your praises to Me and dancing in adoration on My behalf. Your singing, prayers, and cries pierce from the depths of your soul that waits expectantly with excitement for My return. As you are waiting and do not forget, may My spirit fall on you with My promises, joy, peace, love, forgiveness, and hope. As you receive these gifts, then go out and share them with everyone. I tell you to delight, delight in everything and these words that I give you to say:

I am going to delight in the Lord in all my circumstances, delight in the Lord in everything that I do, delight in the Lord in all my relationships, delight in the Lord for unanswered prayers, delight in what is to come even though I can't see or understand it right now.

Exodus 35:10; 1 Peter 4:10

Beautiful One,

I have seen your challenges and struggles in your daily life. I want to let you know that this is temporary and part of the healing and transformational process. Use this time to reflect on these challenges and what I may be trying to reveal to you about yourself. Do not be fearful or resist this process. You are already equipped with an untapped resource of an innate intuition, an instinctual drive, and spiritual clarity that will allow you to touch the depths of your soul as well as others. Spend quiet time with Me so that I can open a space within you that will allow you the ability to creatively express the work that I am doing in you to create harmony within you and around you. As others watch you grow by being stripped and transformed, they too will be affected. Embrace letting go of the old self, and surrender to Me by allowing Me to make life changes that will bring forth hope and opportunities that you could never imagine. I will lead you, and you shall follow.

Psalm 32:8; Mark 8:34–35

Beautiful One,

I see your heart for others as you quickly jump in to help them out no matter their circumstances or situations. You have great courage and loyalty to all those with whom you are in relationship. I encourage you to use your faith as well to pray for those with whom you come into contact. You can do this silently unto Me. I also ask you to pray and forgive yourself. I have heard those prayers, but I now ask you to claim that prayer in the name of My Son, Jesus Christ. By His stripes, you are already healed and forgiven. You are quick to pray and tell others that they are forgiven and not to look to the past; but you sometimes stand as though you are on a high cliff, and you waver back and forth in that truth. Claim that truth, and do not let the enemy deceive you into thinking anything else. If you can claim this and hold on to it, it will release you and set you free. You will feel great relief in My honor. This freeing up will allow you to be more equipped to heal souls. You have to claim and believe it in yourself first, though, that I do and I am who I am.

Matthew 6:12; Luke 23:24; 1 John 1:9

March 14

Beautiful One,

Another way that I reveal myself to you is through dreams. Pay attention and begin to write your dreams down as soon as you wake each morning. Each of your dreams has significance and meaning about a part of you that is trying to come forth from your unconscious to your conscious. This inner work opens up a whole new experience with Me that will put you in touch with your higher divine or wise self. You will be amazed at what I can reveal to you through your dreams. It takes discipline to write them down as soon as they happen, though, because if you don't, you will forget them. Keep a dream journal and pen beside your bed. This is a way of experiencing My mystery of what is within you that is trying to be birthed and come forth if you will allow it.

Joel 22:28–29

March 15

Beautiful One,

I sense your confusion, mixed emotions, and sadness that you are moving in a new direction away from your comfort zone of surroundings, friends, and family. Sit back and relax like you are on a scenic mountain drive with Me, looking at the shadows of the trees, in awe of the rock ledges, crossing streams flowing freely, and viewing the majestic mountaintops. I am taking you on a romantic journey through My creation by My hands. Don't forget that you too are My creation, and during this time, I am revealing to you the beauty that surrounds you each and every day, while also letting you experience My feelings for you of how beautiful you are inside and out. Don't ever think otherwise. I knew you before you were knit in your mother's womb. I created you to be wonderfully and beautifully made in My image so that you could do great works in My name. Enjoy the journey, and you will be amazed where you end up at the final destination. It is more than you can even imagine.

Matthew 6:33; 28:20; 1 John 5:13

Beautiful One,

I see your deep pool of tears and hurt. You are experiencing feelings of rejection, mistrust, hurt, and abandonment, feeling used and all alone in this. This is temporary, My sweet one. This time will pass, I promise. Realize how important and beautiful you are in My eyes. I have great hopes for you in the future. I have an outpouring of love for you that you can't even begin to understand. You have one of the most kind and giving hearts of anyone that I have ever known. I am pleased that you always put your feelings aside for others by serving their needs and forgoing your own. Be patient, be quiet, be still, and let go of control, and let My Spirit work in and around you. This is part of the healing plan and grace that I offer you with an unconditional love, Beautiful One. I know right now it seems impossible that the hurt will subside. I do have something significant planned for you, and you will experience my joyous harvest that is coming. Trust, delight, and be faithful so that I can show you how I work for the good of those who love Me and serve Me selflessly. Your tears are not for nothing. I see every tear, and each one has a blessing that is coming your way. You are not alone, and you have not been rejected. You can trust that your hurt will go away. You have not been abandoned, nor have you been used. The enemy only wants you to think that. Stand firm against the enemy. I am with you.

Psalm 31:9; Romans 8:28; Ephesians 6:11

Beautiful One,

I see you growing stronger in Me. Even though you don't understand everything right now, I see and hear your thankfulness in all of this. I want to encourage you to keep doing the next thing that I may direct you to. It is also important for you to get out and travel some, and enjoy movies, hikes, the outdoors, reading, and cultural experiences so that you can continue to grow stronger in Me. Enjoy simple pleasures because we still have much inner work to do together. This is the beginning of you experiencing the power and energy that only I can fill you with to complete you into the person I intended you to be. Now the work must begin.

Psalm 105:1; 106:1; 107:1

Beautiful One,

I see all the wounds and scars on your heart from the past. These wounds can also shape you into being a better person. For instance, your insecurities have made you an independent, responsible, and reliable person. Your early losses of relationships make you treasure each and every encounter and realize that it is for a moment in time and not to be held and controlled. Your lack of resources has given you a strong work ethic and drive to provide. Your time of crisis has given you empathy to care and share your resources with others when they are suffering. Your kind and gentle nature has evolved out of these circumstances that I have used to shape you. From these experiences, you have gained knowledge and wisdom that there is going to be pain and suffering in life, but there is also meaning and purpose in it. Your faith is unwavering, and you know that I am always present in everything.

Matthew 21:21; 1 Thessalonians 1:3

Beautiful One,

You are in a valley again, but I am here with you. I have full-force winds blowing around you, coming in all directions. You are not in harm's way, but this experience is one of blowing and using My Spirit to move you to where I need you to be in order to get you to stable ground. Once I have you on this stable ground, My transformational work can begin to blow away the things of the past so that you can start fresh and anew. I know this place where you are feels like you are isolated on an island in the middle of the night with no light visible at all. I see you. I am here. This is where I can do the most work within you, when you are at this place. Sit in this place and with the painful memories because there is light within you that is getting ready to burn bright. I know there is so much internal conflict going on, but believe and trust My process because you will come out from this dark place balanced in every phase of your life.

Genesis 1:2; Romans 8:14

Beautiful One,

My heart hurts with your heart. Just keep breathing in and know that I am the one who supplies your every breath and what you need. I count and hold all of your salty tears that are streaming down your face. Meditate in My presence, and I will speak into you. You are almost there, Beautiful One. You are being directed onto a new path that is going to broaden and enlighten you. With everything that you are carrying, it is going to be possible to complete in My strength. I have not led you this far to set you up for failure. You are now standing on a solid foundation that is setting you up for knowledge, inner wisdom, success, and passion. You have such courage to continue on this path, and it will lead to positive changes in your life that will ultimately give you freedom. Trust that these changes are for your good in every realm of your life.

Job 27:3; 33:4; Isaiah 42:5

Beautiful One,

I see your frustration and feeling of being stuck where you are. You have a lot of heavy emotions on you that you do not need to carry by yourself. Simply slow down, meditate, and unwind by releasing your emotions and thoughts to Me. As you release these emotions and thoughts to Me, pray that you can surrender it all to Me. Once you can surrender, that is when the healing can begin. I go before you and behind you, blessing you with My presence always. I have rescued you from harm, and I am making you anew. Trust and believe My ways and My will for your life. When My work is complete in you, you are going to be transparent so that My light can freely flow from and through you for all to see. You think that your struggles and inability to surrender show a sign of weakness and failure. I see your diligent efforts, and you are making progress toward healing. Don't give up, and continue to surrender each and every thing that you can. It will get easier, Beautiful One.

Psalm 23:3; 34:17–20; 2 Corinthians 12:9

Beautiful One,

I desire to have one-on-one time with you today. Come and meditate with Me outdoors in My beauty. In this stillness with Me, you will receive My peace and the way of holiness. This highway will be your direct path to righteousness and Me. Do not fear or be alarmed at the wicked along this path. You are protected from them because I am with you every step of the way. I want you to trust Me and to also trust yourself because I already dwell within you, which means that you are always close to My comfort and peace. Speak positive words of love and praise into yourself. Let Me awaken your mind, body, and spirit so that you can know the person I created you to be in My Son Jesus Christ's name. As you become rooted in knowing who you are in Christ, you gain My wisdom, My thoughts, My ways, and My unfailing love.

Psalm 139; 141; 143; Isaiah 35

Beautiful One,

I am directing you on a new path, but you question My decision for you. There is a part of you that feels and knows this calling, but there is also a part of you that has reservations because this is taking you out of your comfort zone. Allow this new journey to broaden and enlighten you. I know it seems like an overwhelming task, but I have called you to this time and place, so be disciplined and follow My lead. I will make your time and resources abundant to meet your needs. These life changes will bring you knowledge, inner wisdom, success, and passion that will be used courageously to serve others with positive life changes. Many opportunities will be available to you within My timing. Trust and believe that these changes these changes will be for your benefit as well as the benefit of others.

Psalm 23:1; Isaiah 30:21; 43:19;

Beautiful One,

Do you realize that you are My beloved child whom I divinely created with a special purpose? Because I am in you and you are in Me, I give you My love, faith, hope, joy, and peace. Through my Son, Jesus Christ, you have been reconciled, and I want you to experience what that fully means. You have already been forgiven, and you have My healing. I give you freedom in Me with My grace and mercy. If you simply pray and believe in what you ask for, anything is possible through the anointing of My Holy Spirit. I want you to experience My abundance of being connected in mind, body, and spirit, which gives you an unshakable character and whole being. This is the bliss of heaven on earth that I want you to experience.

1 Peter 5:5–11; 1 Thessalonians 5:16–18

Beautiful One,

I have a message of truth for you today. I know your burdens and trials are really heavy and overwhelming right now. I see and count your tears. Your tears are for a purpose and are part of my plan. Each tear that you shed will come in the form of a blessing. Continue to have faith and trust in Me by doing the next thing. Don't look too far ahead; don't look to the past, but keep your focus and eyes on Me. I am shaping and transforming you into the person that I intended you to be from birth, although your circumstances and choices have gotten you off the narrow path that I prepared for you. Now you are on the narrow path, and I am almost done with My work in you. You are almost there even though you can't see it yet. Don't give up.

2 Chronicles 15:7; John 17:17; James 1:18

Beautiful One,

A joyous harvest is coming your way so that you can have the peace, wellness, and wholeness that you have so desired. You will be a blessing to others and equipped to walk them through their pain just as I have done with you. You are a beloved child to Me in whom I take delight. I am so proud of all the hard inner work that you have been doing. Continue to keep your eyes and focus on Me, trusting in Me always. I have been right beside you the entire time, even when you didn't feel My presence. I was quiet so that you would seek Me more. Keep seeking Me; be still and listen for My next message to you.

Psalm 126:5; Galatians 6:9; Hebrews 12:11

Beautiful One,

Just as a farmer diligently prepares the soil of his garden, I also prepare your heart to receive and nurture the seed that I have planted within you. Once the farmer has planted his seed, he waits patiently for the day's light to get longer and warmer so that the seed can burst through the dark soil. I also work within you in the same way by planting desires within you that require patience on your part to be in that dark place within yourself before you see what I am birthing in you. My timing is perfect and will not be too early, nor will it be too late. Trust in My ways and the process, and you will experience an abundant harvest in the next season. During this process, praise Me continually, even when you don't see the harvest. Once you see this harvest to fruition, continue to praise Me and honor Me by letting others know of My great work in you.

Hosea 6:11; Luke 10:2; John 4:35–36

Beautiful One,

You are a beacon of truth standing firm on a solid foundation, like a lighthouse beaming out its bright light for others to find and come to Me. It doesn't matter what the weather conditions are, because through the storms of life, the fog of confusion, or the twisters of the enemy, your light is going to continue to shine so that all can see. No matter what the circumstances are, speak My truth; speak boldly and courageously on My behalf. There is no need for fear or worries, because I am the light that is in you, protecting and assisting you along the way. Continue to walk on this spiritual path that is leading you to your divine life purpose and mission.

John 9:5; 8:12; 2 Corinthians 3:12

March 29

Beautiful One,

I created you with a divine purpose to believe in Me first and foremost. Examine all areas of your life, and ask yourself if you are believing in Me in all areas of your life. If you are not, you are missing out on receiving the eternal life and abundance that I offer you. Ask Me to search your heart and reveal areas that you need to believe in. Don't let the enemy deceive you into rebelling against Me. If you rebel against Me, you do not believe in Me. You are going to use your hands as if they were Mine to serve others, which will glorify Me. I just need you to trust and believe in Me fully.

Proverbs 3:5; Jeremiah 29:11

Beautiful One,

I see your tears, pain, and sickness in all of this. You are letting the enemy control and enter your thoughts. I know you do not like feeling this way. Come to Me and ask Me to take over the thoughts of your mind. I want you to rely solely on Me. I want your intimate dependence on Me. I am here, ready to help. You just need to invite Me in. Give this struggle to Me, and I will give you peace and blessings.

Genesis 50:20; 2 Corinthians 10:5

Beautiful One,

The more spiritually mature you become, the more you will be a witness to My work here on earth. You are becoming attuned to My nudges, and you are being obedient by going when I prompt you. You are My vessel that is gaining strength and confirmation of My calling upon you. The stronger and more attuned you become to Me, the more you will witness that I am alive, active, and moving all around on earth among you. Keep immersed in My Word and promises so that you can recite My Word at any moment to anyone who is in need of faith or healing. You will be a walking testimony to My promises and love for everyone. Keep seeking Me, and for everyone that you meet, look into their eyes to see Me, no matter who they are, where they are in life, or what they have done. Let My Holy Spirit work through you. Thank you for allowing My loving presence to be within you so that it can pour into others.

Psalm 119

Beautiful One,

You have been flooded with emotions, and this is good. Focus on these emotions to raise awareness in your unconscious of where they come from. It is safe for you to explore these places because I am with you and will bring about healing. For each and every emotion that surfaces, ask yourself if you love yourself unconditionally like I love you. Do not feel guilty or bad about experiencing these emotions. Not only do they stem from the present situation, but they also relate to pasts hurts, failures, and circumstances. Your spirit is longing for love. Love yourself first, and then the healing can begin. This lack of love for yourself is an obstacle. My child, you are worthy to be loved, and I have a special plan for you. When you can open your heart to love yourself, you will experience My joy, truth, and happiness that no other relationship can give you. Love and forgive yourself just as I love and have already forgiven you, Beautiful One.

Proverbs 19:8; Ephesians 5:29; 1 Peter 4:8

April 2

Beautiful One,

I see you and feel your heartbreak, but I want you to lift your head up high and acknowledge Me. Listen to Me. There is nothing from your past or in the future that will keep Me from loving and accepting you. Don't let anxious or unworthy thoughts enter your mind. Let go of the feelings of shame that have made you feel used, unloved, and disrespected. I know it is hard to accept why those that you trusted would make you feel like this, but you are more than your circumstances and choices. The only thing that matters is that you know I love and accept you as you are, where you are. Continue to seek Me; your security rests in Me alone, which will affirm who I intended you to be, giving you comfort and peace. I have glorious plans for you, so stop clinging to these thoughts and old ways. I am doing something new in you, so move over and allow Me to show you what is in store for you. No longer will you feel weak and abandoned. I am making a way in the desert and streams in the wasteland. You are going to be like a rose in the desert springing up where no one thought possible. You will marvel at what I have done in you.

Psalm 56:34; Isaiah 43:19; Romans 8:38

Beautiful One,

I know you have been seeking answers, and I am going to reveal the truth to you no matter how painful it may be, because the truth will set you free. I am putting others into your life who are going to need your assistance, so all of your pain and suffering has not been for nothing. Not only will you counsel others in helping them to heal, but also they will teach you lessons of internal things that you need to work on and refine. Pay attention to each and every relationship that I put before you. It is not a coincidence, but part of My plan that the relationship be a blessing to you both. When you embrace this, there will be freedom and peace in this process that will allow My Spirit to work in you in an unobstructed way. I am in control of every situation in your life, and I am also with you through thick and thin.

Psalm 115:3; Proverbs 16:9; John 8:32

Beautiful One,

Demonic spirits are again trying to enter your thoughts, making you anxious, fearful, and distracted. I want you to envision Me encircling you with a beam of radiating light shining upon you. Feel My warmth enveloping you. This light has brought you out of darkness, free from shame and unworthiness. Feel My presence radiating upon you with unconditional love, delight, joy, and respect. I am protecting you and keeping demonic spirits away from you that are trying to pull you away from the peace and contentment that I give you. Don't fall for the enemy's lies, and keep your focus on Me by meditating and praying each day. I am pleased when you don't feel like spending time with Me but do it anyway. The more you do this, the more it builds up your faith and trust in Me. You have been called for a special purpose and duty. Keep doing the next thing, and soon I will reveal My plans for you. Fulfill My plans by giving up control, because your plans have serious spiritual dangers ahead if you don't let them go. Trust Me.

Proverbs 21:1; Zechariah 4:6; 1 John 5:19

April 5

Beautiful One,

Things seem shaky for you right now, and you are wondering what is going on in your life. I am shaking things up in your life so that the hidden and dead parts within you can be released. I am doing this out of My love for you and ask that you just trust Me and this process so that this oppressive burden can be stripped away. I am releasing the chains and shackles that have continued to weigh you down and hold you back. I see your weakness and woundedness, but just know that My light is shining upon you so that you may experience My healing grace. Stay in this place where you are. I will show you My work and glory through you. I am unfolding and bringing forth the things that are destroying you within, such as your pain, suffering, bitterness, unforgiveness, guilt, loneliness, anger, pride, shame, and mistrust. As the tent unfolds from within, bringing light to these hidden sins, I, the all-sovereign God, will unfold love, peace, joy, hope, faith, compassion, unity, wisdom, truth, knowledge, ministry, counseling, altruistic service, and trust. This unfolding is painful, but look at the beauty of what is within you when you surrender to Me to bring all this forth.

Isaiah 54:2; 2 Corinthians 5:1

April 6

Beautiful One,

Your inner being is developing within like a beautiful flower of radiating colors that is starting to bloom and show. It still holds some sadness, but the flower is pushing it out of the way. The beauty can no longer be held back by weak inadequacies. As the flower pushes out to reveal its new growth and petals, it is an inspiration of hope and opportunities that are unfolding. These opportunities are bursting out and becoming greater. Around these opportunities are pure fun and amazing experiences. It is also a mysterious and synchronistic spiritual experience, giving you inner strength and energy. Rest, be still, meditate, and be content with this process so that each flower petal opens in My perfect timing in an effortless way. There is so much beauty here within you.

Psalm 103:13–18

Beautiful One,

You have hurt others in the past. All you have to do is pray and ask for forgiveness for things of the past, but more importantly, forgive yourself. I have already forgiven you, so extend the same grace for yourself by forgiving yourself. This will free you and open up opportunities that have been blocked by this bondage. Surrender your plans and desires, and trust Me. Don't get stuck at this place. My sight, My plans, My ways are higher than any of your thoughts. This season of your life is coming to an end. I can now bring you new opportunities that you never imagined possible. Healing is near, but you must completely surrender and release what you have been clinging to. You will be an influential example and leader for others by exhibiting inner wisdom and spiritual maturity to them. I am affirming that you are on the right path, and you will serve and love humanity in a capacity that you never imagined.

Isaiah 55:8–9; John 4:24

Beautiful One,

I am working on giving you a gracious, nonjudgmental, flexible, and spacious spirit and attitude. Search and examine all of your interactions with others. Today I convicted you of sometimes having a rigid spirit, where you act and say things in a way that you never noticed until today. You can sometimes say and believe that only your way is the right way of doing something. Now that this hidden sin has been revealed to you, I am giving you a spirit of softening your heart and a new way to be with people and encourage them by loving them where they are. I will calm your overbearing ego. Your openness to hear this and act on it will bless you and others. This process strengthens you and gives you great inner beauty of compassion, empathy, kindness, graciousness, and altruism. Slow down and be with Me more, and I will keep revealing to you the qualities that you have that are like My Son, Jesus Christ. You are becoming unshakable.

Psalm 19:12; Proverbs 28:13; Isaiah 29:15

Beautiful One,

Don't choose to stay stuck and in your comfort zone. If you do, you are living blind. You can't even begin to see right, physically or spiritually. Reflect on the past of what did not work, and don't stay with what is familiar even though it may be painful, fearful, habitual, and sinful. This place is stagnant and does not challenge you to live by faith and in My perfect will. Become radical, and experience the ambiguity of being in relationship with Me. There is a new realm if you are ready to experience Me fully. When you accept going into the next realm, I will work for your benefit in your trials and pains, but I will also possibly lead you away from familiar friends, relationships, work, and areas. Be ready to move where I lead you to go. It may be permanent, it may be temporary, or it may be a test to see if you truly are ready to take Me seriously and experience My supernatural power. How badly do you want to experience Me fully and what I have ordained for you? Ask for My anointing and power. I want to give to you fully. There is an amazing vision that I want to reveal to you. Will you get out of your comfort zone?

1 Timothy 4:12; 2 Timothy 2:15; James 1:22

Beautiful One,

Celebrate today and where you are. I know your circumstances are not ideal, and you have much hurt, pain, struggle, and great loss. Reflect on where you were in the dark, but now there is light that is getting brighter and brighter. Thank Me for things getting better, instead of criticizing Me. You may not always be able to notice, but things are getting better in your life. Ask Me to touch and anoint you for what it is that you need right now. Don't turn to worldly relationships, possessions, finances, or status to fill you with things that are impermanent. These are only temporary and will set you up for failure again. If you seek these things, you are walking blind and will continue to fall victim to these circumstances. When you are comfortable with Me filling you, you are going to feel safe, at peace and at home. It will take work to stay at this place so that you don't fall back into the patterns of the past of sin, habits, pride, and attitude. Stay free in Me, and live life with abandonment and without restriction.

Isaiah 42:67; 61:1; Luke 4:18–19

April 11

Beautiful One,

You have had the pleasure of experiencing My presence surrounding you by feeling My Spirit of wind around you. Breathe in the wind because it is My breath that fills you and gives you energy and movement. My wind also carries you by directing you and transforming your path. It is an opportunity for growth and something new getting ready to be born from My Spirit. Don't resist My path and new direction for you. Let go and let it be. I know this is a continual internal conflict for you. Embrace My energy that is within you, full of truth and light that is trying to come forth. The old ways and things that you are holding on to are your false self or old ways of being. No matter how much you cling, strive, or hold on, My divine inner strength is coming forth, and in your weakness, you can no longer repress Me. Don't resist the process, and let go, sit in the stillness, be patient, love yourself, forgive yourself, and let Me, with all of My loving-kindness, unfold the mysteries for your life that are in My perfect will and purpose. New fruit is ready to be birthed. Let it come forth.

Psalm 89:17; Isaiah 66:9; 1 Corinthians 1:27

Beautiful One,

No matter where you have been, where you currently are, or where you are going, I am with you, protecting you. I am your Savior. Praise Me for your challenges, transformation, and growth. I know sometimes it seems overwhelming, but remember that I don't give you more than you can handle. I just want you to fully surrender to Me and go through that door. Don't just stand at the door and be comfortable, but go through the door so you don't miss your gift and new opportunities that I have for you. Don't question or doubt, and just walk on through with courage. Once you walk through, close that door and don't look back. Part of this walk is also being fully present in the moment, paying attention to what I have surrounded you with, such as the sky, the sunset, the birds, and certain positive and encouraging relationships.

2 Samuel 22:4; Psalm 63:4; 86:12

Beautiful One,

I know you believe that this process is going slowly, but I am building a firm foundation under you through this transformational process. This process is sure and steadfast to make you unshakable. This is necessary to grow the beautiful inner treasures and gifts that you possess so that you are prepared to pour them out to others. Your past sins and story are part of the bigger testimony that has brought you to this point that is ready to be exposed from the cocoon, like a butterfly that is getting ready to fly to new opportunities, a new way of being and doing. During this process, you have gained much wisdom and have become transparent. You are getting ready to develop in a new spiritual realm where all things are going to be possible through Me. Others are going to see your resiliency, inner beauty, creativity, hope, compassion, joy, peace, wholeness, and loving-kindness. Others are going to be drawn to you and will want to experience and know how to experience this spiritual fullness. You are going to make a difference in many lives, giving them a freedom that they have never experienced.

Isaiah 61:1; Romans 8:1–2; 2 Peter 1:2–4

Beautiful One,

There is a part of you that is carrying around something that you don't like, and you continue to cling to it. Let Me tell you what I see. I see a beautiful gemstone within you that you won't claim. You are ignoring your birthright of who I created you to be, as well as your creativity. Gemstones endure much pressure in the depths of the mountain which makes them powerful, perfected and with few or any infractions. It is no mistake; the month you were born is your birthright gemstone. Claim it and embrace what it represents. Be patient with yourself and the process that is taking place even though it seems like your prayers are not being answered.

Galatians 3:29; 1 John 2:6

April 15

Beautiful One,

Follow and trust your divine inner calling that I have placed in you. Let go and abandon all of the false parts of yourself. Once you completely surrender all to Me, you will recognize and hear more of My whispers. Your steps will no longer be your own, but of a higher purpose and will. As I continue My transformational work in you, you will gain purity, clarity, and wisdom. This will allow Me to use you to be a light to others so that they too may experience My love, peace, wellness, and wholeness. Your steps and life are no longer your own.

1 Corinthians 6:19–20; Galatians 2:20

April 16

Beautiful One,

    I am equipping you for a church ministry. Keep in mind that this ministry will not be what you think of as a church. Part of your work is to continue to do your own inner work and to be vulnerable with sharing your process and your story. I know your ambivalence of doing so, but your transparency is going to speak intimately to others to also become transparent and do their own reflections.

2 Corinthians 3:1–6; 12:9–10

Beautiful One,

I know you are feeling mentally, emotionally, and spiritually drained. Stay close to Me with continued praise. Spiritual warfare is fierce right now, so do not let the enemy have control in this situation. Pray and come to Me continually; Give Me your fear and suffering so your heart does not harden. Allow Me to soften and open your heart. Do not resist the process. That is what the enemy wants. When you come to Me, you open your heart to Me and invite Me in, which allows Me to whisper and have a dialogue with you. I also give you the bodily experience of feeling My warmth and peace. My warmth and peace are a balm, releasing the pain and suffering to one of feeling loving-kindness, compassion, and healing.

Exodus 33:14; Psalm 16:11; 95:2–3

Beautiful One,

Just know that I am doing a new thing in you. I know it is painful. I have seen your tears and suffering, but you must solely rely on Me. There is so much spiritual warfare going on around you that it is trying to distract you, so it is even more important that you keep focused and in communication with Me so that your thoughts and actions don't get you off the path that I have already so lovingly directed for you. Each day, I want to spend this type of quality time with you so that I can comfort you and give you instruction on this new, exciting path that I have planned for you before you were even conceived. Don't allow the enemy to distract you, make you feel anxious, or confuse you. Give yourself to Me completely and freely each morning before all these distractions start to burden you. I can give you all you need in order to walk in My plan and direction for your life, but you must first come to Me with an open heart and open mind. It can't be your plan, your wishes, or your desires. You still need to completely surrender.

Job 11:13–15; Isaiah 43:18–19

Beautiful One,

I have seen your efforts, and that is good; but when you are not certain or feel like you need to fix something, you go your own way of trying to force it and do it in your own strength. You then show Me that you don't need Me, that you don't trust or believe in Me fully. I want all of you so that I can use you to show you and others My glory. Come to Me and only Me. Let Me show you each and every step that I have so lovingly created and orchestrated. You just have no idea how amazing and exhilarating it is going to be, but I need you fully and completely in order to fulfill My plan. It honors Me when I have you fully present by spending one-on-one time with Me.

Mark 10:28; Galatians 2:20; Hebrews 11:6

April 20

Beautiful One,

You are still scared, and the fear that you are experiencing is what keeps driving your anxious thoughts. Take the next step by coming to Me and letting Me take away your fear. Don't question, cling, or try to make everything perfect in your plans and timing. Rely solely on Me and not others for answers, affirmation, or recognition. I am using this time to let you be assured of who you are in Christ. That is the only assurance you need. My assurance is unfailing. You have exhibited courage by stepping out of your comfort zone. You have exhibited strength even when you didn't want to continue. You could have easily stopped and given up, but you didn't. You have persevered. You have shown your willingness to open your heart and hear My voice and whispers. Not only that, but you have discipline and obedience with only a few reservations, sweet child. These are the qualities that I equip a warrior with to do work in My kingdom in order to show My glory. You are precious to Me, and I am so delighted in the work you are personally doing and the work you are going to do for My kingdom. Don't ever give up. Look to Me always, and rely only on what I tell you about who you are in Christ. All things are possible through Me.

2 Thessalonians 3:13; Hebrews 10:36; 12:1–2

Beautiful One,

You are more than a conqueror. I recognize and feel your timid and anxious emotions. I am glad you are aware and recognize them. Meditate in My presence by breathing in deeply of My spirit of newness in you. When you exhale, release the negative feelings and emotions, repeating that you are praying for peace and wellness not only for yourself, but also for others who may be experiencing the same feelings and emotions as you. I love it when you come to Me with your emotions, body-felt sense, and struggles. I want to be your everything in every situation. I want to show you that I am always with you and that only I can give you peace and wellness. There is nothing in this world that can fulfill and give you that. You are starting to spiritually mature in your relationship with Me. As a result of this, you are going to see My greatest works and glory be revealed to you in a way you could never imagine. There is no earthly friend, relationship, or possession that can even begin to touch what I can offer you when we are in divine union. I want to share this with you, My child, so keep pressing in closer and closer. This delights Me greatly. I am constant. Will you be constant in our relationship?

Ephesians 4:1; Philippians 1:27

April 22

Beautiful One,

As you awaken this morning, you recognize your warm bed but feel cold, nervous, and anxious. Stay in this place by meditating in My presence so that I can give you insight into this transformation that I am leading you through. It is a necessary process for you to feel this pain and suffering so that you can gain compassion, loving-kindness, and empathy for others. It is a time of softening your heart, making you fully aware and present of others' suffering as well. You must experience this so that you too can minister to others that I put before you so that you can walk them through the healing process. This pain and suffering is also stripping away false parts of yourself, your clinging tendencies, and your holding on to relationships, possessions, and the past. This is a death of your old way of being, the false parts of yourself and the overinflated ego that took you a lifetime to develop. Once I have stripped away all of these false parts of yourself, I will reveal to you the person that I intended you to be before you were even conceived. I already had a plan for you before you got sidetracked. Sit in the unknown and be completely vulnerable to where I am taking you.

John 12:24; Philippians 3:8; 1 Peter 4:1–2

Beautiful One,

Things of this world are impermanent. That is your lesson. Your trials, hurts, and pain won't last forever, but be grateful in them because they are strengthening you and teaching you to grow in a way that would not have otherwise been possible. The lesson to gain is not to cling or hold on to relationships, family, blessings, or possessions. Be grateful in the moment, and fondly treasure the memories while realizing that none of it is yours to hold on to. It is for a time and purpose, and you must be willing to love it at the moment and then be prepared to let it go as you grow from each for the next thing I have planned in your life. If you cling and stay at this place, you will become stagnant and stuck where you are. That is not what I want or have for you in this life. I want you to continually grow strong within yourself, but also within Me. I want you to experience everything that I have prepared for you, but you have to be willing to keep moving and to keep paying attention to My nudges and My whispers so that I can reveal to you who you are in Christ. Just keep taking that next step in faith, and be content even though you can't see the end. My plans for you are to prosper you and not harm you. I am going to use you to show others My glory that is all around them. You are going to be My light that is shining forth My truth. Let your light shine, and I will quicken and prepare you for what you need. Trust and believe, Beautiful One.

Ecclesiastes 3:1–11

Beautiful One,

Draw near to Me and let My face shine upon you like the beaming, radiating sun. Draw near to Me and let Me put My loving arms around you with a firm embrace, but with gentle care. Draw near to Me and let Me take your worries of this world so you can rest securely in Me. Draw near to Me and I will heal your broken heart before you even know what you need. Draw near to Me and I will fill you with joy and peace, a way of being that only I can give. Draw near to Me and take delight in My ways. Draw near to Me and I will give you your heart's desire. Draw near to Me—I am calling you, Beautiful One.

Psalm 65:4; 145:18; James 4:8

Beautiful One,

I know you are questioning who you are in Christ. Let Me assure you that you are not those negative or self-critical thoughts that you continue to have. That is not of Me. That is your overbearing ego driven by the enemy telling you that you are not worthy, that you are not doing enough, or that you are not doing things correctly. These thoughts block or become an obstacle to a free-flowing and radiating relationship. It blocks the love that I am radiating upon you. It blocks the self-love, self-care, loving-kindness, and grace that I want you to experience. You have to have self-love, self-care, loving-kindness, and grace for yourself so that you can be My light and radiate this to others. This is the gift that I give you. I want you to experience this fully. Then this gift you must share and give to others. It is not yours to hold. This gift is not impermanent like other things you sometimes seek. Continue your self-reflection with gentleness, and grow from what I reveal to you. I am nudging and encouraging you. Never will I be critical and self-damaging to your being. I created you and know you. I want you to be who I intended you to be. I want you to fully experience My love, grace, and loving-kindness. Beautiful One, you are worthy to be loved and at one with Me. This is not a selfish act, but one of necessity so that you can be fully present and love others from a radiating, higher divine inner self that invigorates you and lets others experience a love from Me that radiates a warmth like they have never felt before and that they seek more of.

2 Corinthians 5:17; Ephesians 2:10

April 26

Beautiful One,

As you continue on the narrow path that I have called you to, you will experience conflict among family, friends, and others. Don't let that distract you. I encourage you to meditate on Me even more. As you meditate, know that I am in you, and you are in Me. When you get that, you experience My mercy. What that means is that it's not earned, but I give it to you anyway. I am in you, and you are in Me. I am calling you. You doubt and wonder how I could use you. You have been blind and deaf, but now you see and hear. You experience My visceral emotions. I am in you, and you are in Me. Accept losing yourself and what you used to be. In order to gain everything, you must relinquish all by meditating in My presence. I will not let you fall, because I am in you, and you are in Me.

Deuteronomy 14:2; Matthew 22:14; Mark 1:17

Beautiful One,

I am so thankful for our beautiful relationship, and I delight in your wanting to know Me more intimately. I have seen your appreciation for My love and mercy upon you, and I am going to show you how to care and love mercifully all whom I bring to you. You exude warmth and are bursting with My love that overflows. You are ready to give to others unconditionally. I see your growth. You see with renewed sight, you hear with compassion, and your heart feels what others are feeling. I see your humbleness, and I will continue to put people around you who will support and encourage you. I have mighty plans for you. You can't even begin to imagine what is in store for you so that I can show you My glory. Your continued seeking has found Me. Continue to seek Me, and I will reveal even more to you.

Matthew 9:36; 20:34; Hebrews 2:17

Beautiful One,

As you continue to draw closer to Me, demonic attacks will become even fiercer than you have ever experienced. The enemy is really angry that you are seeing, hearing, and obediently pursuing the plan and will that I have for your life. The enemy is trying to shake you by entering your thoughts and emotions. Stand firm and call upon My Son, Jesus Christ, to give you strength so that He can intercede and protect you. He will fight this battle for you so that you can just rest in My peace and presence. During this time, go inward with prayer, gratitude, and reflection. This time of inner work and reflection is extremely important because it is bringing forth the next new opportunity that I have been orchestrating for you. Trust and believe in Me, and take advantage of this time to mature in Me. As promised, it is going to be exhilarating and something that you could not have planned or worked out on your own. Sit back, enjoy, rest, and watch Me do amazing things in you and through you to show you My glory. Your battle has already been won.

Exodus 14:14; Joshua 1:9; 2 Chronicles 20:17

Beautiful One,

Do you realize that you are *free*? Yes, free from the bondages of sin, the past, an overbearing ego, and from the enemy's attacks because of My Son, Jesus Christ. When you are feeling attacks, simply call on My Son, Jesus Christ, and the enemy will have no power over you because Jesus will come to your rescue by pouring His loving presence over you, which is His full armor of protection from the enemy and worldly temptation. It is no mistake that you have been called to be a disciple. You are being called to be a frontline warrior for those who are in the back of the line with no voice, no hope, no vision, or who may not even know My Son, Jesus Christ. I am calling you to be My servant and warrior to lead others to Me. There will be many, and the road may seem steep, hard, and long, but I will place individuals before you that you are to lead to Me. Don't be overwhelmed by all the work or think of how you can possibly help everyone. I am just asking you to be obedient and to minister to those that I place before you. Continue to do your own inner work, which removes your selfish and fleshly habits. It will be as though I have hollowed you out so that there are no obstacles or blocked culverts within you. That will allow My Spirit and love to flow through you like a river.

John 8:32–36; Romans 11:26 ; Colossians 1:13–14

Beautiful One,

You are My chosen one that I have called to be a servant and warrior. I am equipping you to be a hollowed-out vessel that I can pour into, through, and out from with overflowing joy, love, peace, hope, and promises. The peace that I give you will be felt and recognized by those around you. They will be drawn to you, and that will be your opportunity to share My love for them and to introduce them to Me. There will be those you meet who you think are unlovable. You may think they are unreachable, but I tell you and command you to love them anyway. This may be the only time in their lives that they get to experience an unconditional love where they don't need to give anything of themselves in return or be hurt by it. Love, love, love them anyway! It is one of My greatest gifts and commandments that I give you right now. That is why your heart feels so compassionate, warm, and overflowing for everyone you meet. Your compassionate, loving heart has softened the calloused scars. This will be one of your strengths that leads those who are deeply hurting to Me. I am leading you, Beautiful One. All you need to do is follow each and every step of the way because I have already prepared and equipped you for this calling. You will lack nothing and be abundantly blessed by others.

Luke 6:27–36

Beautiful One,

I am so encouraged by where you are right now. You know that you have been called to ministry because you are hearing and knowing My voice. You have created a space that allows you to hear above the noise and distractions. With that, I am well pleased. Your love for Me and others is obvious by your acts of kindness, interactions, and hugs for others. I created you to have hopes and desires. These hopes and desires are to draw you closer into relationship with Me. I know the enemy sometimes tries to trick you with other hopes and desires, but you first and foremost must concentrate on Me. I must be your first hope and desire, and then I can unfold My plan for your hopes and desires to show you My love and glory so that you can be My vessel to bring others to Me. I have seen how hard you have worked, and I have heard all your cries to Me. This process of hollowing you out from all the dark places within is necessary and painful. This process will allow Me, My Word, and My promises to flow through you like a radiating light where there is no darkness, no hesitation, or obstacles. Beautiful One, I am using you to let My truth shine through you like a beacon of light sparked with so much energy that nothing of this world can extinguish it.

Matthew 5:13–16; John 8:12; Romans 13:11–14

Beautiful One,

Your mind and thoughts are racing this morning. Stop and meditate in My presence. Don't allow the enemy to control your day in this way. If you do, you will be easily distracted and taken off the path I have directed for you even before you knew it. Do not be blindsided by the enemy's deceitful ways and schemes. Sit in a comfortable position with your eyes closed. These thoughts that are present for you, place them in a box one by one. Shut the lid to the box and tape it securely. Now move the box to the side. Focus on your breaths as you inhale and exhale. With each inhale, breathe in new thoughts from Me that will draw you closer to Me. As you exhale, release any negativity or things you need to let go of. Keep repeating this process until your mind is clear and you feel relaxed all over. Take it a step further and breathe in a prayer for what you need. When you exhale, send this prayer out to others who may need the same thing. Keep practicing that and notice what comes for you. Spending time with Me and being in My presence is the only way to calm your racing thoughts, relax your body, and give you the peace that you so desire. Do this with Me each and every morning and experience your day in a new way. Allow Me to go before you, behind you, and with you. You don't have to do this alone.

Psalm 1:1–3; 19:14; 104:34

May 3

Beautiful One,

You don't think so, but I want you to know that there is beauty here in this place where you are. When I asked you to take up your cross, I asked you to deny yourself of personal wants, desires, and plans. I asked you to follow Me and live out your life purpose and calling. I know it often feels lonely and empty, but that is an opportunity to come to Me to allow Me to fill you with My joy and peace. You often think if you had a significant relationship, a certain job, looked a certain way, earned a certain amount, or had more that you would be happy and fulfilled. I caution you that this is the enemy setting you up and deceiving you. These are empty thoughts that are going to let you down even when you attain them, which will make you feel like a failure. Then the cycle starts all over again of wishing you had more, you could do more, and the "if onlys." When this cycle or these thoughts begin, come to Me with these thoughts and ask Me to replace them with My thoughts for you. Let Me tell you who you are in Christ. I will never tell you that you are a failure, you need to do more, or you need to earn My love, grace, and mercy. When you come to Me, I am so delighted, and what I want you to know most is that you are a precious daughter to Me whom I love very much. Just be in continual prayer and meditation with Me because My Son and I have already made the ultimate sacrifice so that you can spend eternity with Me. It is nothing you can earn or even deserve, but I give it to you because of My unfailing love for you in all of your circumstances. Accept that, and just be in My presence with gratitude because I have rescued you and set you free in My Son's name.

Isaiah 61:1–3

Beautiful One,

I still see and know that your heart aches for the things of the past. I am in the midst of all of this with you even though you don't understand or like this feeling. You put so much emphasis and focus on the past that you lack vision of what I am doing in your life. You take two steps forward then one step backward when you accept these feelings of longing, emptiness, and loneliness and ask where they come from, what they are trying to let you know, why they are so overbearing. These are parts of yourself that you must acknowledge and have a dialogue or conversation with in order to see what they reveal to you. Also, come to Me and spend time with Me so that I can reveal to you the next thing that I am orchestrating in your life. I promise you that it will be good. I do want to give you your heart's desires, but you must do it My way in My timing. You are not ready, nor are you prepared yet for what I have for you.

Psalm 11:10; 147:5

May 5

Beautiful One,

I have prepared the pathway for you, leading and directing your steps. You intentionally cannot see the final destination. I am asking that you take one step at a time. You should be on guard while you are on the path because there will be many distractions that will come your way. I tell you to stand firm in your faith, being courageous and strong. Diligently pursue this pathway that I have prepared for you so that you will experience joy, optimism, inspiration, and growth. I will show you My peace, clarity, and love. The spark is within you that is getting ready to ignite within you and out to others. I am preparing you on a solid foundation, enabling you to achieve the goals and aspirations that I have placed in your heart. Work harmoniously with yourself, others, and the universal energies put before you. I am supporting and encouraging you along the pathway and ask that you set things in order to move things forward.

Luke 21:34–36 ; 1 Corinthians 16:13

Beautiful One,

I am with you, and I give you My reassuring words that you already have the strength within you to stand up and walk out of those chains that have been weighing you down. No longer will you feel depleted, sad, hurt, hopeless, worn out, or tired of feeling this way. Your feelings of loneliness and difficulty have been a necessary process in order to prepare you for the next thing. You won't know the exact outcome, but just know that it is part of the plan and that you must hold onto My divine inner wisdom that gives you strength. I am surrounding you with support and won't leave you during this time. Embrace this time and experience so that you will be equipped and ready for the next thing that is on the narrow path that is just right around this next turn. When you get close to the next thing that I have prepared, that is when emotional upheaval and turmoil overcome you. Know that it is the enemy who is trying to do everything in his power to keep you from making this turn. Keep pressing forward, eyes on Me. Focus on quiet time with Me so that you hear and know your calling. I know the pain you are experiencing, but I have something amazing birthing from this pain. You are almost there!

Psalm 28:8–9; 103:2–3; Luke 5:31–32

Beautiful One,

We have been at this place before, and here we are again. You are trying to manipulate and control your outcomes by being in your comfort zone. Ask yourself if you have really surrendered all to Me. At this point, I don't believe you trust or rely on Me in all of your situations. Be on guard because the enemy is coercing you into these emotions and reactions. Your anxious thoughts and fear of losing someone so dear to you is what is making you sick. When you are sick like this, you pull away from Me, rebel against Me, and stop meditating in My presence. That is what the enemy wants. I know this is not what you want. You have come too far to turn away right now. I don't want you to turn away. Press in closer to Me so that I can show you what is around the next turn. You are so close, and that is why the attacks are fierce. I know your heart and desires. I am going to reveal and give that to you in My perfect and ordained timing. Again, trust and believe that I know the perfect peace, the perfect time, and how this will all unfold. If you linger with Me during this time, you will be fully equipped and prepared to be fully present to be the best you can possibly be on My ordained journey for you. I don't want you to miss it because of your human nature in lacking patience and wanting fulfillment immediately. This pain and suffering is going to allow you to appreciate this time and relationship in the most profound manner. Be patient and wait upon Me.

Matthew 11:28; Ephesians 4:31–32; 1 Peter 5:7

Beautiful One,

You have been in a very dark place, and I want you to know that I am with you. When you go to this place, call upon Me. I will surround you and work on your behalf through healing grace to strengthen and inspire you with that fiery-spark warrior that is within you. You are like a precious gemstone that has been in the dark refining process, and you have just been mined and intricately perfected by your choices, challenges, and sin. Yes, this is a painful process, but one that is necessary and daunting at times. Sometimes you have to go to those dark places and sit in them so that there are no infractions to the gemstone. This mysterious unfolding process is at the core of the divine, and it can seem overwhelming. It is overwhelming because your ego clings to and tries to control its simplistic ways because of its ignorance and lifetime stronghold on its way of knowing and being. Once your ego is stripped and shattered, your beauty, light, creativity, love, and compassion will overflow out of you and into others. Don't sidestep or try to take any shortcuts from this process because here in the deep inner soul is where wounds are being healed. Your heart is being softened, and you are giving loving-kindness to all you interact with and meet. This is a gift you are giving yourself and also a gift that you will be leading others to for healing. You are emerging into a strong, altruistic, powerful leader with humility. You are going to be one of My frontline warriors leading the way.

Psalm 12:6; Isaiah 43:2; 1 Peter 1:7

Beautiful One,

My grace is always present with you wherever you are, showering you with My love and offering you compassion and a space for you to be still so that you can hear and acknowledge those groans of your soul that is seeking healing and wholeness. I will never leave you alone. When you experience that dark place of feeling sick, anxious, internal shaking, fear, cold inside and out, and very restless, understand that it is your soul's way of shaking and awakening that buried place that your ego has been controlling and hiding. The wrestling that you are experiencing is necessary so that your soul can groan and break away from the grip of years of rusted wire that has had a stronghold on this part of you. This time is necessary, but it can be overwhelming and scary as well. Trust and believe that I am with you and that you are safe. I encourage you to embrace this process so that you can continue to become pure and whole so that you will have an unshakable ability to be with others in their darkness to help guide them to healing, grace, peace, and wholeness. You have shown much courage to endure this process, and I see your humility and gratefulness. Continue to look deeper and deeper within so that I can reveal to you the greatest mystery and the fullness of My power that resides within you.

Isaiah 48:10; Daniel 11:35; 12:10

May 10

Beautiful One,

You are beginning to see parts of My plan for you. Everything that you have done thus far has led up to this point, and I am going to use it all. I am preparing you for a ministry to be with the lost and broken. You will give them hope so that they may experience dignity, self-worth, love, and healing. I will make the way for you, providing everything that you need: resources, business, knowledge, networking relationships, and finances. I have prepared you to be with the lost and broken by loving them and honoring them so that they see Me. Rest and rely on Me, and I will show you how. Just keep doing the next thing that I put before you. That is all you need to know for now.

Job 23:10; Isaiah 25:6; Malachi 3:2–3

Beautiful One,

Do not go before Me. All of this is in My perfect timing. I will reveal to you the next thing. I just wanted to give you assurance that I do hear your prayers and requests, so I revealed to you that everything that you have done up to this point has a reason and purpose that will be used according to My plan and not yours. More than five years ago, your heart was not right, and you wanted to start a business for all the wrong reasons. Now your heart is right, and I have surprised you that this is part of My plan. I had to strip that desire away from you so that you would move where I needed you to be so that I could purify and heal your heart and have you abandon an overbearing ego. You have so many diverse talents and gifts that are going to allow Me to make all of these ventures possible through Me. You have opened your heart to My will and have shown your obedience. Wait upon Me to show you how, and I will not let you fall. Through you others are going to witness My glory by your trust and faith. There is lots more coming!

Isaiah 49:3; Isaiah 62:3; Hebrews 1:3

May 12

Beautiful One,

I see that you are prepared to recklessly serve Me because you have experienced My endless love and opportunities that only I can give you. I now see your subservient heart, and your presence is a light to everyone that you encounter. You have been tirelessly ascending to get to the top of the mountain because that is where you will receive My revelation, just as Jesus was transfigured on the mountain and where Moses met God. The mountaintop brings transition, vision, and sacred revelations. There is much potential that is ready to come forth from the depths of the mountain if you continue to ascend and do not give up.

Matthew 17:1–13

Beautiful One,

I am upon you and so close to you this morning that you may experience trembling all over. Just sit, rest, and be with Me so that you can experience My warm radiating light upon you and around you. It is My gift to you this morning. My love and warmth are flowing from your heart throughout your body. Just sit and receive it. I am refilling you with this love because of your giving and loving nature toward others; you need to be refilled by coming to Me. I will refill you with My love and peace so that you are fully recharged to go out to serve and love. Because My light is so apparent in you, people are automatically drawn to you to receive your warmth and love. They look at you and see nothing but love. That is because of Me dwelling so close to you. Beautiful One, I am working through you so that we can prepare a way for others to come to Me. It is tiring and exhausting, so pay attention to your body and give it what it needs. I have called you and commissioned you, but I also ask that you come to Me each day to thank the work that has been done. More importantly I ask that you rest in My peace. Always come to Me, and I will refuel you and give you peace. I love you, My child.

Ephesians 3:19; Philippians 1:11; Colossians 2:9

Beautiful One,

What are you doing to yourself? You need to let go and let it be. Move on! You are trying to control this situation, but you are making things worse. Let Me work this out for you. It is like you don't trust what I have planned for you or think that you are greater at figuring things out than I am. That is frustrating to Me. Please, I tell you to be patient and let things work their course. If you back off, you will see things My way. They will shift and work out like I have planned, which is for the greater good. You can't understand or comprehend the way that I am working things out right now. Trust and believe by letting go and letting it be.

Psalm 103:7; Isaiah 43:19; Colossians 1:28

May 15

Beautiful One,

I want you to rest and stop trying to figure out every detail. You are making yourself sick, and it saddens Me. Give all of this inner work a break. Let go of the past so that I can work it all out. Enjoy life, and be content where I have you. I do still want you to meditate with Me each morning, though, so that I can speak words and plans into you. Be sure to spend quiet time with Me. You are so special. I want you to have peace and know that I have it all worked out My way. For now, you need to continue what you are doing where you are. I know and have seen your heart and struggles. You have come so far, so please don't allow the enemy or your ego to take you back to those places of fear, insecurity, and anxiousness. I really do want you to be at peace with this process and trust what I am doing. It's not always going to be pleasant on this path, but it is necessary. Remember, I am all-seeing and all- knowing.

John 10:15; Romans 11:33–34; 1 Corinthians 2:10–11

Beautiful One,

You have strong faith, especially for others when you are boldly led to go and have healing or intercessory prayer for them. Have this type of faith for yourself and your circumstances. That is the impatient part of you that I am refining. You need to learn to sit in the stillness and wait for Me to unfold your prayer requests. You will see and understand what I have done in My perfect timing, and you will be in awe with thankfulness and gratitude. Sit back and keep doing the next thing that I put before you. I do want you to have your heart's desires, but it has to be done My way, in My timing, and in accordance with My plan. Enjoy the present moment of each and every thing that I put around you. I am equipping you to live with acceptance of what the moment is and to live within that fully. Part of that is surrendering all to Me. Find joy in each and every task that is before you, regardless of what it may be. Lastly, as you start to accept and enjoy each and every day, there will be this vibrant energy of enthusiasm that will flow in and through you, giving you divine visions that are part of your will, purpose, calling, and ministry. Again, trust and believe. I do hear your prayers, and I do know your heart's desires because I placed them there when I made you. I had to have you at this point to see if you would be obedient and accept the calling that I have for you. Thank you for being obedient, because many will never walk through the door and fulfill their life purpose that I have placed or given them. I am grateful for your obedience and willingness to serve Me. You will be rewarded with your heart's desire in My own timing. I love you, child.

Exodus 19:5; Psalm 18:44; Jeremiah 7:23

Beautiful One,

You are awakening into a new dimension of knowing your true self as well as growing strong in your faith by remaining in the present moment with Me as I gradually reveal things to you. At this place, you will experience My peace, which will allow Me to fully pour My light into you so that others will notice and receive this light from you. As you continue to grow into your true self, you keep your shadow parts in balance, your ego is diminished, and you don't project emotions or feelings onto others. Your truth in yourself will be My light that will reflect into each and every one that I put before you so that they too may experience becoming true to themselves. Beautiful One, this is how I am working in you to be the light of your inner true self and to the truth in Me and My Word so that others can be set free just as I have set you free. Rejoice and delight on this adventure and ministry that I am orchestrating before you. The seed within you has always been there, but you have kept it dormant for so long with your own plans and desires. Gradually it is being rebirthed and coming alive as you are ready. I have fully prepared and equipped you to fulfill this planned ministry I have for you. The time is near, and I promise you it will be an exhilarating experience.

Psalm 16:11; 84:5; 2 Corinthians 2:14

Beautiful One,

Don't fret or worry about how you are going to find the resources, the place, the people, or the plans to put this ministry together. This is not your work, your plan, or your glory to be mastered. This is My plan that I will unfold in My perfect timing, and you will have everything that you need fall into place right before you. That is My promise to you. I just ask that you continue to do the next thing that I put before you, enjoying the journey by being present in the moment. Both the journey and the uncertainty are My gift to you so that I can reveal what I am capable of doing through you by your simply surrendering and giving it all to Me to unfold. I can't wait to see your face in awe as you humbly fall to your knees and weep at what I am allowing you to witness and carry out with Me. It is not as far in the future as you may think. It is around this next turn on this very narrow and steep path that you are ascending. I know sometimes it seems impossible. I know it seems like the air is getting thinner as you ascend higher, and I know it can get really lonely on this path; but this is preparing you to solely focus and rely on Me. I need to know that in the uncertainty you will come to Me, because as more is revealed to you that seems absurd, I need to know that you are going to solely rely on Me. I just marvel in your beauty, in your inquisitive nature, and in your love, trust, and faith for Me. More importantly, I marvel in your deep loving and compassionate heart for others. As you have lost yourself on this journey, you have actually found yourself in Me, which comes with much empowerment, enthusiasm, and healing energy. What an adventure we are on together!

Jeremiah 33:3; 2 Timothy 4:7

Beautiful One,

Come to Me this morning and meditate with Me. I want to fill you with My peace. My peace will dissipate your aching heart, racing thoughts, and longings. Instead, long to draw closer to Me, to know better My ways, My Word, and My promises. Only I can give you peace. Nothing in this world can replace or be greater than knowing and being filled with My peace. When you dwell on the past, it is like walking in a fog in which you can't see or think clearly. It becomes an obstacle, and you miss out on the simple joys, beauty, and opportunities that I have in front of you. Come to Me and ask Me to show you how to release the past so that you can be fully present with Me. I want you to enjoy each and every moment with enthusiasm because that is the gift that I give you in the moment. The destination is important, but I want you to experience Me fully with enthusiasm in each and every aspect of your life, not just for yourself, but for others to see in you what I offer and give to those who love and follow Me. Let go and surrender all to Me so that you can enjoy the abundance that I have for you—the abundance of fully experiencing Me in mind, body, soul, and spirit. This is heaven on earth that I give you, connecting mind, body, soul, and spirit with My peace. You are heaven sent.

Psalm 18:32–36; Isaiah 57:2

Beautiful One,

I am refining your thoughts and feelings so that you will have My pure thoughts and feelings. I notice you getting anxious as you hear this. There is still a part of you that is resisting this final process because you cling to the past and what you had. That is not possible. I can't make things new unless you let go of them. You are being your own obstacle and making the process harder and longer than it needs to be. I will never fail you or lead you astray. I have your best interests at heart, so I just ask you, Beautiful One, to rest in My arms with assurance, surrendering this to Me. I will hold you and comfort you during this time. If you can do this, I can reveal to you the next opportunity that is around the turn, but I need to know that you are solely relying on Me and have given up on the past. I need you at this place so that I can be assured you will listen and discern each and every instruction that I am going to be giving you. If you do this My way right now, you will see My plan unfold effortlessly before you without any distractions or delays. Beautiful One, I want to reveal to you My plans for you. I don't like to see you hurting or struggling. Come, come to Me. I am all you need.

Psalm 46:1; John 16:33; Romans 8:6

May 21

Beautiful One,

I give you this quote to repeat often to yourself so that it comforts you, keeping you from getting distracted: "Stay so close to Me that you lose sight of everything else you see." There has to be an integration and union of you and Me. It is aligning your conscious and unconscious psyche with My will and My Spirit of truth. In order to conjoin these together, you must be more intentional by meditating with Me so that I can create unity with all the parts of yourself. Meditation with Me brings harmony with the shadow parts of yourself, allowing your full potential and creativity to be released. I am awakening the beauty, love, and passion that are within you and that are of Me.

Psalm 65:4; 145:18; Hebrews 4:8

Beautiful One,

The internal trembling that you are experiencing is Me within you so close upon you. Continue to be still and meditate with Me, and enjoy the radiating warmth that is flowing from Me into you. Rest during this time as My Spirit continues to work miracles in your life. You can't see or understand My ways and what I am putting together for everyone to see what I have done in your life. When My plan is revealed and put into action, others are going to see Me clearly in all the workings of your life. They are going to know that it is not by mistake that you have been chosen to carry out My work here on earth for all to see. You are going to be My hands and feet that I know I can trust for this mission to be carried out. You have shown that you are listening, recognizing My voice, and obediently doing the next thing that I guide you to. Stay in My presence, and surround yourself with trusted spiritual leaders who can continue to help discern and encourage you on this journey. Just know that you are not alone. I am carrying you, and you are surrounded by the Holy Spirit and angels. Call upon them at all times. All you need to do is ask, and they will affirm or direct your way if you are ever unsure. Don't ever doubt why I would choose and use you. You have a spark of passion and action within you, but it is not yet time to unleash it. I will let you know when you are to go. Let that spark and passion continue to get fueled with My divine energy that is unfailing and everlasting.

Isaiah 6:8

Beautiful One,

Come and spend quiet time with Me. Breathe in deeply and let My loving-kindness, wisdom, healing, love, and grace fall upon you. I want to give you more of these qualities, diminishing your overbearing ego. Where the two of these meet in union is where a whole new realm of spiritual experiences and blessings can be released into you so that you can be a positive influence to others, making a positive difference in the community and the world at large. I want to gift you with supernatural experiences. Let Me guide and lead you so that you can experience Me in a new spiritual dimension. I want you to see, hear, feel, and know all that I have for you. I want you to bring healing, peace, and wellness to others. You will be My hands and feet to transform a community into one of loving-kindness, unity, and transformation. I am excited that you are allowing Me to lead and guide you, fulfilling the vision that I have laid upon your heart. You will be in awe once you see how I manifest this into reality. You are My beloved child, and I am so delighted in the work that you have done.

Deuteronomy 18:9–13; Amos 3:7

Beautiful One,

My hand is laid upon your shoulders so that you know I am near, comforting you and giving you peace. Keep pressing in closer to Me, and listen for My gentle whispers of affirmation by spending time with Me in meditation. Keep drawing closer to Me so that you can hear and know your next steps on this journey that we are traveling together. We are becoming one, and you are beginning to have an unwavering trust and faith in where I am leading you. No longer do you question or doubt My plan for you. I see your excitement about the mysterious journey, regardless of the destination. This is when you can experience Me fully by living a life full of joy, peace, and abundance. You are realizing that only I can give you this type of enamored life that the world of relationships, possessions, job, and status never fulfills. Worldly desires are shallow and empty in what they offer and give. I, however, give you the fullness of experience of heaven on earth and will in an effortless way give you your hopes and desires before you even really know what they are. Let go even more of your desires and fear, and watch what I can bring to fruition in your life, far exceeding your expectations and plans. Oh, how I have longed and desired to be at one with you in this capacity. Keep drawing nearer. There is more, Beautiful One, that I want you to experience.

Psalm 115:15; 121:2; 124:8

Beautiful One,

The very things that you think you see as truths in this world are not. The only truth that you can experience and receive is by drawing closer to Me and waiting for My whisper to you about which are the truths. The closer you get to Me, the more intimate we are in our relationship, and I can reveal more and more truths and visions into you. Do not be mistaken or sidetracked by what you hear or see, because the enemy is trying to manipulate you anyway possible in order to shake you. When you lose sight of everything you see in this world, it will not move or shake you, causing you to go into emotional turmoil. My promise to you is that the closer you are to Me, the more I will continue to lead and guide you on My ordained path for you with an unshakable faith and trust in My provision for you. At this point, you do not have the capacity to see or know My ways, so just stay close to Me, and I will give you more knowledge and wisdom, allowing you to become virtuous. Just remember, the things of this world are not as they seem. I will show you the truth and satisfy your desires when the time is right. We have more work to do together.

Psalm 119:160; John 1:1; 14:6; Ephesians 1:13–14

Beautiful One,

Crawl onto My lap so that you can hear the whispers of My work for you today. Come and just be with Me so that I can do exceedingly and abundantly in you that you could never comprehend or imagine doing in your own strength. Just rest and be still, allowing Me to carry out My provision for you in your life. I will give you exactly what you need at the appropriate time, and you will have no doubt that it is from and of Me. This longing that you have been feeling has been necessary so that you would rely completely on Me. You had to be completely empty to seek Me more. Now I have purified you from your thoughts so that you can experience My peace and holiness. Lose sight of everything you see by staying close to Me. Don't give up or turn back on the work you have done. I see your obedience, courage, and efforts in My name. There are changes taking place in you and in others that you can't even comprehend. All of this is interwoven together like a thread in a tapestry of My master plan. Trust that I am fulfilling My plan in your life, and you will experience your heart's desire when My work in you and others is complete. Let go, let go, let go, and let Me!

2 Chronicles 15:7; Psalm 28:7; 31:24

Beautiful One,

Your tears and internal fluttering do not stem from a feeling of being overwhelmed and fearful. Rather, it is a feeling of gratitude and thankfulness for My rescue of you. It is a feeling of something significant welling up inside you that you know is coming forth and is very near to being birthed. I am so close to you that it is like a river of life flowing through you that you have never experienced before, and you don't know what is happening to you. I assure you, everything is okay, and it is going to be well. You are experiencing My everlasting love for you with humility. Everything that you have been through, I am returning to you with blessings. Oh, the time is so near, and you have this feeling of knowing it. It is so apparent that you are excited but also humbled that I could lead you, guide you, and have such an intimate one-on-one relationship with you. This is all I have been longing for, and though you didn't know at the time, this too was your longing. When you were completely empty and depleted, you sought and found Me. Now, because of your obedience with your relationship with Me, I can start to show you bits and pieces of what we will be doing together for My kingdom. Draw even closer to Me by meditating and praying each day. I can reveal more and more to you. The vision I have for you is so big that we must continue to go deeper, become more intimate, and grow closer.

Psalm 18:1-10; 16-21; 71:2; 140:1

May 28

Beautiful One,

You are the chosen one that I have called to set others free. The same gifts that you see in others are also within you, waiting to be released. I am pouring My love into your innermost depths, restoring you completely. The tears that you are shedding are part of the restoration process. I have seen your tears and struggles, and it has not been for nothing. I am going to bless you sevenfold, just as I did Job. I am with you and birthing something new in you with a desire for My will. There will be radical steps and actions that I will ask you to take. I know this vision and ministry seem absurd, but this is the plan that I ask you to entrust and carry out.

Isaiah 43:1; Matthew 22:14; Luke 18:7

Beautiful One,

I know you have experienced great losses, but look where you are. You have grown so much over the past several years into a beautiful child who has embraced looking at why worldly goals, plans, and desires shattered and fell to pieces. It hurts Me when My precious one must endure this pain, but when you can stay at this place and honestly examine all the parts that make up who you are, good and bad, you will begin to recognize these bad parts of yourself, where they come from and how they have affected your past relationships and way of being in the past. This process is refining and interacting with all of these parts, and you are becoming full of unconditional love, grace, and compassion, not only for yourself, but also for others. I have witnessed this within you, and it is so beautiful, the person you are growing to be. There will be no hidden agendas, sins, or desires, but only My thoughts, My plans, My will, and My desires that I am placing upon your heart. At this place, coupled with your faith, courage, and My will, I am going to be able to exceedingly and abundantly cause a glorious ministry outpouring from you that will reach many hurt, broken, and spiritually depleted souls. I am paving this path for you even though you can't see the progress that I am making. You tend to get impatient and aggressive with wanting to move forward with your plan, but I caution you to wait upon Me. I am placing the right people and preparing the resources that will be necessary to get this vision implemented and running effortlessly so that you can do what you do best. That is to love and minister to others, fully empowering them to know who they were intended to be in My name's sake, which will give them purpose, meaning, and salvation and restore dignity, confessing Me as their Lord and Savior for coming and rescuing them. Each life that you touch and transform in this way will multiply tenfold by the people you serve, the resources you receive, and the facility that will be built and equipped to serve and love all My children. I am so proud of your devotion, relationship, and obedience to Me. I love you, precious child.

1 Samuel 12:24; 1 Thessalonians 2:12; 1 Peter 4:2

May 30

Beautiful One,

It is by no accident that you are here at this place surrounded by women of different cultures, but with similar soul desires as yours. You are abundantly feeling My presence in this space and becoming one, especially with the women that you have met so far. Your souls are connecting for the common purpose to heal, empower, and touch women's lives to give them a hope and a future despite patriarchal and cultural oppression.

And how ironic that you met Francine—beautiful, soft-spoken Francine, who bears the same name as your middle name. You looked into her eyes, and as she shared her love and heart's passion with you, your souls connected. Just in the few minutes that you met her, you saw beauty in her resiliency to overcome the effects of war, her drive to better herself and become educated, and her soul's desire that I placed on her heart of wanting to start a school to educate and give opportunities to the youth in her country. You connected by My presence in body, mind, soul, and spirit. This connection is to affirm what I am doing in your life, to pay attention to the vision and desire that I have placed on your heart. It is no mistake that I revealed these women to you to let you know that you also have these traits within you. Even though you are from very different backgrounds and circumstances, you see that I do place hopes, desires, and visions on My chosen ones who spend time with Me and respond to the calling that I have placed upon you them. This is part of the training and equipping process that is being interwoven into My plan for the vision that I have put before you.

Psalm 55:14; Acts 2:42; 1 John 1:7

Beautiful One,

Your internal tingles and radiating warmth are My confirmation that you are right where you are supposed to be. Keep close to Me, and just keep doing the next thing that I put before you. My timing is never too early or too late, but always perfect. Your tears are tears of humility and humbleness because I am using you to carry out My divinely ordained vision that will bring so much hope, healing, and unity in this community by you being a light of truth and security for all of those that I put before you. They are going to know Me by your service, compassion, and loving-kindness to them by giving them an opportunity that no one else would grant them. Keep walking by faith, keep in constant meditation with Me, and pay attention to your body-felt sense. This is how you know when I have something to communicate with you. This always has priority over everything else in your life, if you want to stay in perfect step with My plans for you. You now know spiritually, bodily, and mentally when I need your immediate presence. Thank you for paying attention to that by obediently recognizing I have something to share with you. I am your best friend. We share all and confide all to each other. We are true soul mates, and I will never leave, reject, or betray you. That is My promise and truth to you. I have amazing and abundant plans for you to fulfill My glorious plans in My kingdom here on earth. Oh, the heavens and I rejoice that you want to be ever so close to Me and in My presence, serving Me selflessly.

Genesis 13:17; Isaiah 35:8; 2 Corinthians 5:7

June 1, 2013

Beautiful One,

In My presence this morning as you are meditating, take in deep breaths of My newness for you, letting Me fill you with what you need and trusting that I know what that is before you do. Exhale breathing out, letting go of what you don't even know you need to let go of, again trusting My ways for you. As you practice this, your thoughts will become less because you are surrendering to what I know about you that you are not even keenly aware of. Then I put on your heart to reveal to you that no matter what you have endured or where you have been, My hope has been within you all along, like a thread that is attached to you in heaven. This thread and the interweaving of circumstances, people, and surroundings are beginning to be knit together like a perfect tapestry of who you are and what you were called to do. Just keep your focus on each thread, and enjoy where that thread is being placed and with whom. This is the excitement of putting together a tapestry, because you can't see the finished piece, but you know each thread that will fill you with hope and much faith even though you can't see or know My ways. I am completing one of My most prized pieces of work in you. When you see the full vision and final work, you will just stand back and look in awe at how delicately and intricately I interweaved each detail, leaving nothing out.

Psalm 139:13–18

Beautiful One,

When you begin to panic and feel a sick trembling coming over you, envision Me touching your shoulders and feel My radiating warmth and tingling flow down your body. Name what is happening and what you are experiencing, and call upon Me. When you do this, you are getting stronger and are on a firmer foundation of My Word and promises. You are becoming spiritually mature and immediately recognize the enemy's deception and scheme to throw you into a whirlwind. You stood up to the enemy in My name and rebuked the enemy. I am so proud of your courage and strength. This is showing Me that you are becoming unshakable in your faith, and that is a primary character trait that a leader and warrior needs to be equipped with.

Isaiah 40:28–31; 1 Chronicles 16:11; 2 Chronicles 16:9

June 3

Beautiful One,

It is okay, because I am in you and upon you closer than I have ever been. Continue to meditate with Me and breathe in My peace and newness. Each step you are experiencing is a part of the faith journey of being able to hold on and walk through the pain. You are an example to others who know your story. You are an inspiration to others who just simply come into contact with you because of your love for others, the light you project, and the warmth that surrounds you that others take notice of and feel. Be My truth, My light, My hands, and My feet. Stay so close to Me that you lose sight of everything else you see. You are going to be fine because I have equipped you for this appointed time as well. You cannot see or understand what I am doing in you and around you. Just trust and believe, Beautiful One.

Exodus 15:2; Psalm 18:32–34; 2 Timothy 4:17

Beautiful One,

Remember to stay close to Me and not lose sight of Me. That includes your thoughts that tend to go off on a tangent; then you begin to experience emotional and physical disruption that blocks our relationship. Things of this world are not like they seem. I am doing things that you cannot see or comprehend. Keep pressing in so that you can hear and know each step to take and which door to open next. There are going to be many doors of opportunity for you that will open when My timing is right.

Proverbs 4:23, 25; Luke 6:45

Beautiful One,

You are like a boat with tattered sails that has been depleted. I want you to know that I am breathing new life, meaning, and desires into your life that will fulfill you and place you in My perfect will. The deeper you breathe in, the closer I get to you, which makes it easier for you to hear My whispers. This new life and breath are giving you the strength to ascend the steep mountain with the great effort and will that I see on your part. You are focused on moving ahead and never looking back. You are moving in the right direction, and I am so pleased with you. You are right where you are supposed to be. Actually, you are very close to making the turn, and it will then be easy sailing for you. I am not promising you a life free of trials, but I am saying that what you have been stuck with and struggling with for so long is almost behind you. No longer will you struggle with this issue, wishing and wanting that desire. You will not forget, but you will not be at this stuck place. Now you can be in complete synchronicity with Me so that I can fulfill your destiny and My plans for your life. This will be an exhilarating time of creativity and watching My plans unfold before your very eyes. Do you see why this was necessary, Beautiful One? You gave others strength and courage by sharing your story, but more importantly, you released that negative stronghold and energy that you have been trying to carry for so long all by yourself that was in the way of Me being able to move you forward. Now that you have moved beyond the "stuckness" of the past, watch what I do. Sit back, rest, and be in awe of what I reveal to you. It is coming soon!

Deuteronomy 5:23; Joshua 1:7; Philippians 3:13

June 6

Beautiful One,

You are feeling the strength of My power within you. I am so close to you and you are so close to Me that you notice My presence upon you. The closer you get and the more time you spend with Me, the stronger you will become. All of the gifts, characteristics, and qualities of My Son, Jesus Christ, are within you. Spending one-on-one time with Me is developing and maturing those gifts for yourself, but they are also to be used as you interact with and minister to others. Your obedience and self-reliance on Me are equipping you to be a frontline warrior and leader in My kingdom here on earth. You have no idea how great this is going to be and how many lives you are going to change and bring to Me. Press in and get so close to Me that we feel like one; then no circumstance, trial, enemy or event will be able to shake or tear away this relationship. I am your strength and shield. You just need to completely surrender and just *be* by not doing. I will unfold the next steps and open the doors where you are to go. You will witness My works; praise and rejoice in those moments, but also witness with humility. There are many individuals that you are going to be a witness to as well as testimonies to share. Do you feel and know that I am about to reveal something significant to you? I am, so be prepared and be expectant.

Ephesians 4:13–15; 2 Corinthians 7:1; Hebrews 12:2

Beautiful One,

Be still, be still, be still, and know that I am God. Give Me your anxious thoughts and ways. I am doing a new thing in you, so surrender and let go. You can't even begin to see, hear, or understand what I am doing, but I am working and moving in your midst. I am the light and truth, and I am pouring that into you so that you can be My vessel to speak into the lives of others who don't know or have a relationship with Me. Rest for a while and lie at My feet while I do this new thing in you. There is nothing you have to do but just be. Be with Me in My presence. I will give you peace, joy, affirmation, answered prayers, and the next steps you are seeking. Just be so that I can fill you fully and completely to prepare you for this new, next thing. It is so close, Beautiful One. Cling to My robe, and I won't let you fall. We have beautiful work and an amazing journey planned together.

Exodus 14:14; Psalm 46:10–11; Zechariah 2:13

Beautiful One,

You need to surrender more to Me and also this knowing that you have. You are still trying to have control over your situations and outcomes. That is not fully trusting and believing in My works and plans for your life. You have no comprehension of what I am doing, and I have revealed to you that I am going to give you your heart's desire. That needs to be enough for you to trust and believe in Me. I tell you that when you pray and believe, it will be yours. That is My promise. Just believe, have faith, and spend quiet time with Me so that I can reveal the next steps to you. That is what you are to do now. Also, be content here, rest in My presence, be still, and surrender even more to Me. My plans are good for you. I am working all things out for the greater good.

John 4:24; Romans 8:26–30, 37–39

Beautiful One,

You are anxious because you are questioning Me, My plans, and My promises for you. I promise you and tell you that I am a God of truth. My promises have been consistent that you need to believe what you ask for and delight in Me, and then you will have the desires of your heart. It is in My timing, though, and not yours. You don't understand what I am doing to orchestrate this plan, nor will that be revealed to you. My command is to trust, believe, and have faith in all your circumstances by praising Me and giving Me thanks for where you are right now. You are not at that place today. I am nudging you to spend quiet time with Me. I want you to experience each and every day to the fullest in all circumstances because it all is part of My work in you and others in order to fulfill My plan for you as well as your heart's desire. If you already had everything that you have prayed for, you wouldn't get to see My glory in how I will orchestrate it all to mysteriously unfold. I can't wait to reveal it to you when you least expect it. You will know in that moment that it was of Me, and it will be honorable, pleasing, and affirming that I have answered your heart's desire. You will then see My way and why it had to be My plan and not yours. Beautiful One, don't get discouraged or resentful. I do have your best interests at heart while answering your prayers. What a beautiful thing I am doing in you, and I so cherish your obedience and discipline to follow Me and My ways, even when it seems so lonely and tough. I am here with you every step of the way. I love and adore you greatly, My precious one.

1 Corinthians 9:24; 2 Corinthians 4:8–9

Beautiful One,

I am making things new in your life. You must not look back or remember the things of the past. This is creating a lot of unnecessary hurt, pain, suffering, and grief for you. The things of the past before you were in relationship with Me were in your controlling efforts and sinful ways. You must trust and believe that I am working all things for your good as long as you surrender and let Me show you My purpose and will for your life. I am refining and restoring you, Beautiful One, to your birthright of who I intended you to be. You are like a precious gemstone that illuminates majestically that can be seen by others with your love for Me and your love for them. I have refined you in the fire, which has caused you to seek Me more. This firing process cleansed you of your sins and made you pure and radiantly beautiful. It is by no mistake that you resemble a gemstone, because it represents healing for yourself and others, increased wisdom, protection, peace and sacred rest in all circumstances. I am mining you like a gemstone to make you immovable and unshakable in your faith, and I am building you on a solid foundation so that you can carry out the ministry vision that I have placed in your heart. This will all mysteriously be unfolded in My timing and strength, and you will praise Me for this new path I have embarked for you. This new path will bring about self-realization that will fill you with a wholeness and joy of life that you have never experienced before. Beautiful One, you are a rare, precious, and priceless gemstone to work in My kingdom. I can't wait to reveal My plan for you in bringing others to know Me.

Isaiah 43:2, 19; Romans 8:28

June 11

Beautiful One,

You are doing exactly what I want you to do. You are taking one step at a time in educating yourself, immersing yourself in new experiences, and having fun with others in a way you have never experienced before. Continue to laugh, have fun, and explore new experiences. Being able to relax and have fun is going to be important for you to make a part of your weekly schedule because when your ministry unfolds before you, you are going to take off running and will need to have these fun outlets for your personal release. Keep laughing, keep smiling, and keep doing each absurd thing I put before you.

Psalm 5:11–12; Philippians 2:3–5; Philemon 1:7

June 12

Beautiful One,

I do hear your prayers and see your obedience to Me where you continue to do each and every thing that I put before you. It pleases Me that you are fully trusting in Me alone. Trust and believe that your heart's desires will be answered in My timing. Be patient and wait upon Me, as I am orchestrating the outcome in a way that you can't see, comprehend, or even recognize at this time. You are trusting and delighting in Me, and you will be blessed with abundance for what you have so patiently waited for. Continue to wait upon Me, and it will be perfect and more than what you could have ever imagined possible. Use this time to live life fully each day no matter what you are faced with. This is part of My plan to strengthen you with a boldness of courage so that you are My frontline warrior to carry out this vision I have placed upon your heart. This process touches and teaches you in your inner depths, giving you knowledge and wisdom to respond always in a Christlike manner. I am making you immovable and unshakable in your faith. You will be on My solid rock foundation where a ministry is built.

Genesis 29:20–28; Psalm 37:4; Matthew 16:18

Beautiful One,

As you spend one-on-one time with Me this morning, notice the sound of your breaths as you inhale and exhale. The inhale and exhale ebb and flow with the energies of the universe. The inhale is like a wave from the ocean that is coming in with newness, and the exhale is the wave that is releasing all that is within you that you have been clinging to. Keep breathing and visualizing each breath as a wave that is coming and going. That coming and going is also Me, My energy that is within you allowing this process to happen. As the strong waves come and go, it is strengthening you but also giving you peace and rest. My gift that I give you right now is peace and rest as I bring in each new wave of newness and help you to release clinging thoughts, feelings, and desires out to the vastness of My ocean where these things are consumed and engulfed and no longer seem too big or too hard to let go of. I will take them out to the ocean for you and toss them around, swirling them with new people, relationships, desires, plans, and vision for your destiny. The ocean is full of many fish and opportunities. It is all for you to seek and have. All you have to do is continue to be open by spending quiet time with Me, inhaling and exhaling the waves as they come and go. Can you now smell the saltwater? Can you now hear the ocean waves? Can you feel My strength within you? Can you now feel the calming joy and peace it brings to you? Look at life as an ocean of waves coming and going; the coming and going would be people, relationships, circumstances, and trials. This will give you strength to be like the waves that are moving effortlessly with the natural energies of the universe. Can you just visualize that you are that wave? Sometimes the waves may be really big and may crash, but hold onto the peaceful, soothing sound and motion that comes and goes. I am right there riding the wave with you as you release all of this into the vastness of My ocean for something new and beautiful that also gives you peace and rest. I have depths in the ocean that no one has ever seen or discovered. There are depths and opportunities in you too that you have not seen or activated. Keep allowing Me to ebb and flow with new waves of opportunity, releasing old waves from your grasp so that your full potential can be revealed and released. Just as there are places in the deepest and darkest depths of the ocean floor waiting to be discovered, much creativity and potential lie hidden in the deepest and darkest places within your soul that I want to release and bring forth. It is yours if you will fully surrender to this process and let Me show you.

Job 26:13; 32:8; 33:4; Psalm 18:15; Acts 1:8

Beautiful One,

You have been equipped with so much potential to be used in My kingdom here on earth that you haven't even begun to utilize. I have been waiting for you to get to this point of surrender so that you would allow Me to reveal to you the vision and potential that have been unused. You have been comfortable with what you know and have been trying to cling to things of the past. This has been an obstacle to releasing your creative potential. Now that you have recognized and realized this, I can propel you forward to the next thing with divine acceleration. I am excited about what we are going to accomplish together. Most of all, I can't wait to reveal to you the scope of this plan and how I am going to use your full potential for My glory. Come and receive, and then go and give with humility. I love you, My precious child.

Isaiah 49:3; John 1:14; Colossians 1:27; 2 Peter 1:17

Beautiful One,

I am blowing like the wind in and around you. You don't see what I am doing, and sometimes you wonder if I am even working on your behalf. There has been a divine acceleration, and you are getting closer to seeing what I have planned for you. It has been a slow, painful process, but one that has been steadfast and everlasting. I am building you up with strength and bold courage to be a frontline warrior who is standing firm on My solid rock foundation. My foundation is solid, and it has been spoken over you that you are on the right path by others who don't know you and those who have questioned you. It has been spoken in truth, and now the enemy has no entryway to discourage or threaten you. You are My anointed one with spiritual gifts and hidden potential that are going to be released in a supernatural way that is going to propel you to the fruition of the vision that I have placed on your heart. When you speak of this vision, you light up with passion, and love flows out from you. That is My indwelling desire, plans, and strength in you that are going to make this all possible in an effortless way. You are going to see blessings and favor for all of the sacrifices you have made over the past few years, because I know that you are also going to give blessings, healing, and love to all My underserved, unwanted, and hurting children. Your loving-kindness and compassion are going to flow out from you onto them, changing their lives so that they see Me and come to know My Son, Jesus Christ. I see your excitement and willingness to sacrifice your life to serve Me. There is great abundance there for you. This church ministry is going to be something radical and new that no one has ever imagined, and I am delighted that you have answered the call. You are close, Beautiful One.

Amos 4:13; John 3:8; Acts 2:2

Beautiful One,

As the wind of My Spirit blows, stirs, and moves things around, I too am stirring and moving in your inner being. I am moving and stirring within you new thoughts, visions, desires, and passion. You recognize this because you are experiencing an overabundance of joy and excitement that you feel like you can't contain. This is just a glimpse of the joy and peace that I am working out to give you. Hold on to this feeling, and wait patiently upon Me to direct your next step and to open the next door. That is your next task: to learn to sit patiently and wait upon Me. I know you are feeling as though you are bursting with ideas and plans, but it is for Me to unfold the vision for you in My strength and timing, not yours. It is My glory to be given and credit to be received, not yours.

Psalm 18:10; 104:3; Isaiah 59:15; 2 Samuel 22:11

Beautiful One,

You have ascended the mountain and made the turn, and now you are on the straight stretch and almost to the finish line, where your church ministry vision will unfold before your eyes. I am excited to see your face with amazement and you bowing on your knees, humbly crying with praise and joy to Me for choosing you to carry out this ministry for Me. You have been chosen because of your obedience to Me, your open heart, your loving-kindness for all humanity, and especially your love and devotion to Me. This ministry is going to be big, successful, and more than you could ever imagine or plan yourself. You are going to bless this community, transform lives, heal souls, reconcile relationships, and create a community based on the foundation of one of My most highly revered principles—*love*. Because I am love and you have Me within you, you too are love. Love conquers all. You are a conqueror, Beautiful One

Psalm 24:3; Acts 2:27; Ephesians 4:8–10

June 18

Beautiful One,

Keep doing each new thing that I put before you. I am guiding each of your steps and each new person who comes into your life in My perfect timing. It is all for a greater purpose, and it will be unfolded before you. I know how hard it is for you to be still and sit patiently, but I have noticed that you are embracing this new way of being. Sitting at this place will benefit you greatly, and you will receive more of My whispers and direction in this place with Me. I am filling you with My anointing to be steadfast, strong, unshakable, and immovable in your work for Me.

1 Corinthians 15:58; Colossians 3:17; Hebrews 10:23

June 19

Beautiful One,

Stay present with Me today, not letting your thoughts go to the past or looking to the future. My gift to you this day is to enjoy this very present day. Each day is a gift that I give you, and I ask you to reflect with gratitude on all things that are put before you. It may not seem like anything significant is happening in your life at the moment, but there are gifts and nuggets of truth in each and every small thing that I put before you. How you cherish the small gifts is a reflection of how you will cherish the big gifts and new opportunities that I am about to reveal to you. Show Me your humility for the small gifts as well as the big gifts that are coming your way. Do you see how the small gifts in the present moment are a way for Me to train and prepare you for the greater gifts? I am all around you in all things. I come in many forms and sizes. Open your eyes, ears, mind, and heart by rejoicing and praising Me in all things this day. I come in small packages, disguised packages, as well as in large packages. The more you notice this, the more humbled you become by all of My creation and the package of all My gifts surrounding you.

Philippians 3:7–16

Beautiful One,

It is true that I am doing a new thing in you so that your heart, mind, body, soul, and spirit are one with Me and Me alone. I am giving you Christlike qualities that will serve not only you, but also everyone that you meet and serve. I am equipping you with the anointing of spiritual gifts and enhancing those that you already have. I have seen how difficult this has been for you, and your struggles. I commend you, though, for sticking with this process, because your blessings will be abundant and overflowing, just as the abundant and overflowing tears you have shed. This process is cleansing you and making you pure while also giving you perseverance, strength, and courage. I am strengthening you physically, mentally, emotionally, spiritually, and socially so that you will be unshakable and immovable in your work to serve others. I will bless you and reward you with more than you could ever imagine possible with your heart's desire, visions fulfilled, and financial prosperity. You don't see it, but there are many individuals that I am placing in front of you who will lead to the fruition and birth of the vision that I have given you. Keep pressing in to Me; spend time with Me, and read My Word and promises. Keep doing the next thing that I put before you, because it is all part of My plan in order to fulfill your destiny. It is significant, so keep pressing forward. In My perfect timing, you will understand My way and why it had to be done that way. I see you, Beautiful One, and you must know that all of this is for your good; never would I harm you. My ways are supreme. I love you for your heart, love, passion, courage, and commitment to Me. With you I am well pleased.

Matthew 5:48; 25:40; Luke 10:30–37

Beautiful One,

It hurts Me so much to see you like this. It is not My intention or plan for you to be in so much pain and to be emotionally drained. Trust and lean into Me when these feelings come up for you. Have confidence that I am working this all out for you. You can't see or know what I am doing for you, but I assure you, it is all for your good and will come in My perfect timing. My plans for you are significant. It is more than the vision that I have given you and more than you can imagine. This emotional conflict and battle that you are struggling with is from the enemy and spiritual warfare. Together in unity, I have already won this battle for you. Don't fall for the lies and schemes of the enemy. He wants you in emotional turmoil to get you off the path that I have divinely orchestrated for you so that you will be distracted and unable to physically, mentally, emotionally, and spiritually carry out this plan I have promised you and your heart's desire. My Word is true and constant. I will not fail you, leave you, or deceive you in any way. That is not My way at all. I am protecting you. Keep calling on Me. I know the fiery darts are fierce because you are so close. Keep fighting, keep trusting, and keep pressing forward because you have My full body of armor upon you with My anointing to do great and mighty things. I am manifesting supernatural spiritual gifts in you and refining and amplifying the ones you already have. You are a uniquely gifted individual who is going to lead like a frontline warrior, but you are also one with an innate unspoken, powerful, compassionate but firm style of leadership that will inspire those who work with and around you to perform and be creative to levels of potential that they never knew existed. Your presence and work are going to be facilitative and nurturing while healing each and every person with whom your ministry works. Beautiful One, don't lose sight of Me. Stay so close to Me that you lose sight of everything else you see. This is significant! I need you focused on Me and the vision. Keep doing each and every new thing that is before you. It is all part of the plan. You will see.

Proverbs 3:26; 2 Corinthians 3:4; Philippians 1:6

Beautiful One,

I have examined your heart, and I know your inner depths. You are letting fear control you and make you feel anxious. Don't let the enemy or your ego deceive and manipulate you in this capacity. You are stronger, and I am with you. Keep pressing forward with the next thing that I have divinely orchestrated for you. You are protected by Me. When you notice and feel fear, rebuke the enemy and call upon Me. Each time you rebuke the enemy, you get stronger and stronger, making the enemy weaker and weaker. This process accelerates the plan and vision that I have placed upon your heart. Work enthusiastically with determination, and know that these attacks by the enemy mean you are on the right path and close to a breakthrough. Oh, we have amazing plans where we will be saving souls, restoring dignity, and building a community of love in the name of Jesus Christ.

1 Chronicles 16:8–13; Matthew 6:25–27; 1 Peter 5:6–7

Beautiful One,

As you sit quietly with Me in meditation, breathe in deeply My Spirit and experience our closeness by noticing how your body feels. You are seeking, and I am so close and upon you. Open your heart to Me even more by asking for My guidance and direction instead of seeking answers. When you ask for guidance and direction, you are allowing Me to direct your way by surrendering to My leading instead of asking for your way. Release your sadness, disappointment, and fears to Me. Those are qualities of grief that you are experiencing because of lost past memories and dreams. Release them all to Me so that there is no obstacle preventing you from receiving and hearing My soft whispers for your next steps. The things of the past that you have lost seem significant to you right now, but I can assure you that I have something much greater for you than you could ever imagine. Fear is the enemy, and he wants you to stay stuck here. Don't settle or stay at this place, because there are great opportunities and abundance waiting if you will take action and put systems into place to fulfill your heart's desire, soul's mission, and destiny. The action and steps that you take in My name will be an example to others who are watching you, whom you will be serving and leading. Stay close and ask for My guidance and direction.

Psalm 10:17; 57:7; 97:11

187

June 24

Beautiful One,

Get away from your situation, your surroundings, and the people who continue to hold you and keep you stuck. This is a warning that if you don't move away from these circumstances, there could be serious negative consequences that will lead not only to your death or destruction, but also to the loss of the vision and your soul's life purpose that I have placed on your heart. You have much potential that I am trying to unfold and birth in you during this transformational process, but it all is being jeopardized by your unwillingness to let go. You must let go in order to see the full fruition of what I am doing, if you want to experience being completely at peace with joy, fulfillment, wellness, and living out your divine purpose and mission. Don't settle for what you think is good here on earth. I have so much more than your heart's desire could even imagine or comprehend. Trust Me, follow Me, and believe in Me that I am working all things out for the greater good, not only for you personally, but also for all those whom you will be serving, loving, saving, and healing in My name. Can you do this? I know you can! But will you choose Me and My way and not your selfish desires? It is your freewill choice.

2 Corinthians 10:4–5; James 1:22; 1 John 1:8

Beautiful One,

The time is now, if you have not noticed that I am opening doors for you. I need you to walk courageously and boldly through each door, staying completely fixed and focused on Me. Things will begin to move quickly, but just stay in constant step with Me, not deviating or doubting each next thing that is before you. Work heartily at each and every detail and task, and watch how I unfold everything that you need in order to make this vision I have placed upon your heart to actually become a realization very, very soon. I have been telling you that it is just around the last turn, and not to give up on it or get distracted. You have remained so strong and steadfast through the enemy's attacks and your personal pain. I am so proud of you, and there will be many rewards, blessings, and abundance for you as a result of your faithfulness and actions. You are going to touch and change so many people's lives, leading them to Me. Every tear, every penny, every heartache, every lost desire—it is going to come back to you tenfold. Your obedience to allow Me to work in and through your life pleases Me, so I will fill your every need before you even know what it is, Beautiful One. Sit back, rest, and let Me continue to unfold and work all of this out for your greater good. It will be more than you can even imagine.

Proverbs 12:26; Matthew 16:23; Romans 12:2

Beautiful One,

Come to My feet this morning and rest before Me. It makes My heart grateful when you come to Me. The more you come to Me, the more I can transform you. I will give you clear thoughts, pure desires, great sight and vision, and an open heart and ears to hear My whispers. When I look at you, I see you perfectly made in My image, with no judgment of where you have been and the wrongs you have committed. The blood of My Son, Jesus Christ, has already washed away all your sins, and I just see a precious child who is going to do many great things in My name. I ask you to see yourself as I see you: a pure, delightful, transformed child who will be seeking and fulfilling the life purpose and mission that I placed on your heart before you were even conceived. Don't let the enemy distract you and tell you otherwise. Stand firm and rebuke those thoughts because I have already won the victory for you in My Son's name. Focus and concentrate on that, and keep pressing forward to fulfill your destiny. There will be much peace, wellness, reward, and abundance at this place. It is all yours.

Ezekiel 36:26; 2 Corinthians 5:17; Ephesians 4:22–24

Beautiful One,

Rest and be comforted that I am with you, guiding, directing, and protecting your each and every step as you boldly and courageously work at implementing each detail, task, and system to unfold the vision to fruition that I have placed on your heart. The time is now to work diligently and obediently by keeping your focus on Me so that you will not be distracted. Your angels are also assisting you to help manifest your heart's desire and soul's mission. You are becoming stronger with renewed energy and passion to carry out this vision. Thank you for stepping out in faith with confidence to lead this mission with grace and nobility in My name. Because you have experienced trials in the darkest places, you are going to shine the brightest to all those that I send to you so that you can minister to them to bring them hope, love, happiness, healing, wisdom, and acceptance of how to enter into the kingdom of heaven. There is already much glorious singing in the heavens because of your commitment, boldness, perseverance, and endurance to carry out this mission and ministry in My name. What a glorious sound, Beautiful One.

Isaiah 40:29; Ephesians 6:10; Philippians 4:13

Beautiful One,

I am filling you with My love so that it will be in abundance to pour out and overflow into everyone that you meet and minister to. That is how others are going to know My Son, Jesus Christ, because of your outpouring love they receive from you. This experience will pique their curiosity, and they will want to seek and know more about My Son, Jesus Christ, and My promises and truths that I have given. Continue walking in faith, and believe even though you can't see the next thing, because your walk in faith keeps effortlessly opening the next door. I have called you to walk on the water, proclaiming My name, and all of your needs, visions, resources, works, and deeds will be met. As I have told you before, I am excited to show you how all of this is going to unfold. You have nurtured the seed, you have worked diligently for Me, and you have trusted and believed that in My perfect timing you are going to reap an abundant harvest. It is close and near that you will begin to see the fruits of the harvest and My Spirit that dwells in you giving you strength, courage, and perseverance.

Psalm 23:5; Malachi 3:10; Matthew 5:6

Beautiful One,

Daily spend time with Me, and ask Me to fill you with the fruit of the Spirit. When you are filled to overflowing with the fruit of the Spirit, it makes it more difficult for the desires and temptations of the flesh to become overbearing. Rebuke the enemy, and overcome this conflict by opening yourself to Me and the Spirit. Abandon your fleshly desires, prune the past sins and negative parts of yourself, and immerse yourself with living water, positive influences, and friendships that will nourish you. If you do these things, the rest will take care of itself, and you will bear much fruit. By living this way, you are set free and liberated. My grace has made this possible, and I only ask that you be in relationship with Me, love everyone, and live joyfully. Let Me have dominion over your life, and you will experience all the gifts of the Spirit. A joyous harvest is near for you to claim and bring in.

Daniel 7:14; Matthew 8:27; Hebrews 1:9

June 30

Beautiful One,

You took a major step today when you finally said good-bye to the past hurts, sin, and pain in your life. When you said good-bye, the enemy lost all of the strongholds and his control over you. You are no longer in the boat, looking to the past and contemplating and looking into the future. When you said good-bye, it was the first step out of the boat onto the water. Now continue to focus on Me, and you will walk on the water effortlessly. You just took another step closer toward your harvest. Can you feel the excitement and expectancy within yourself? This step just opened up another space within you that will allow you to receive your next step and message. Pay attention to all the small details around you and the people I place in your path now. Resources will not be a problem or issue. They will be abundant. This vision is near fruition, and there is not going to be one small or large detail that is going to prevent this from happening. What an exhilarating time this is going to be. There are so many people supporting you and sending you prayers. Your angels have surrounded you with much love, encouragement, and protection as well. You just need to get to this place of not looking back. That door has been closed now. There is nothing impossible for you to do since you are in My complete will. There is so much joyous singing in the heavens today that is celebrating your upcoming harvest. I am delighted with you, Beautiful One.

Psalm 34:7; 91:11; Daniel 6:22

July 1

Beautiful One,

I know it has been difficult to get to this point of saying good-bye to the past and what you know. This is the beginning of a shift within you and of something beautiful emerging. I send you My peace and ask that you claim the vision that I have placed upon your heart. Your patience is increasing, your faith is becoming unshakable, and your light is getting brighter. I see your humbled heart and hear your thoughts of how I could use a poor country girl like you: one born from sin, one who lived with shame and humiliation most of her life, and how you thought you were never good enough. You are My perfect disciple. I have stripped all of that away and restored you. I live within you, and you are all things in Me. Remember, I was the one who conquered giants, parted the sea, turned a few loaves into many, caused the blind to see, healed lepers, released demons, and even raised the dead, including you! You are a new creation and reborn. Hallelujah!

Ezekiel 37:1–14

Beautiful One,

The feelings and sensations you are having are anxious and nervous feelings. You know what you are supposed to do, but you are scared about the finances and how you can possibly do this. I've asked you to trust Me. Give your anxious thoughts and feelings to Me with prayer and petition. Don't let those anxious thoughts and feelings control you and keep you from walking in My perfect will and plan for your next step and life's mission. These thoughts and feelings are not of Me, but from the enemy trying to paralyze you from taking the next step, because when you do, things are going to unfold quickly with a huge impact on you, those whom you will serve, those whom I send to you to be a part of this ministry, and the community at large. This step that you take is the biggest one that you will take in a leap of faith. I ask you to take it. When you take it, it's another defeat against the enemy, and he is losing his grip and stronghold on you. He is grasping at every little possible thing that he can use to prevent this ministry from happening. You are almost there, Beautiful One. Keep pressing in closer and closer to Me. I am with you each and every step of the way. This is My plan, My vision, and My glory to be achieved, so I will not let you fail as long as you continue to be obedient and disciplined with each and every thing that I ask you to do. Once you take this next step, it is another victory, and you will be blessed abundantly. Surrender your small thoughts and concerns to My unfathomable thoughts and ways. You can't even begin to see, understand, or comprehend My ways. Surrender to My will and let Me show you. This will increase your faith and trust in Me even more. I am making you unshakable and immovable, Beautiful One, so that as you lead this ministry like a warrior, you will be unstoppable in saving souls and leading others into My kingdom for eternal life in My presence. With you, I am so well pleased. The heavens and the angels are singing and rejoicing. Keep moving forward.

Romans 5:3–4; 2 Thessalonians 3:13; James 1:12

July 3

Beautiful One,

I see your efforts to jump in and fully surrender to Me and My will for your life. The first step looked huge to you, but you trusted Me and courageously took that next step of faith. As you plunged into the water, you noticed that it felt so good. Even as you were getting out of the water, you were confident, strong, and self-assured with My peace. That is what I gave you as you completely surrendered to Me. No matter what comes your way as a trial, burden, or obstacle, just hold onto that feeling of My presence of flowing water all around you giving you peace. You are experiencing the supernatural energy and healing of My peace and presence that only I can give. You are living, breathing, feeling, seeing, and hearing My Spirit in supernatural ways that come from the heavens and meet you in the earthly dimension. Continue to be still with Me, and you will experience more of My strength, energy, and gifts in a new realm.

Job 11:13; Mark 10:28; Ephesians 5:18

Beautiful One,

Your strength and power are unfolding, and you are feeling liberated, which brings much freedom and creativity. This liberating power comes from looking at the dark and light sides of yourself by accepting and loving them both, creating unity so that one does not become overbearing in a maladaptive or negative way that can cause destruction to yourself and others. Continue to go deeper, unraveling all these parts of yourself, because this process is making you unshakable, immovable, and unstoppable not only in your faith, but also in living out your soul's life purpose and mission for My kingdom. You are going to do many great works and deeds that will outlive your life but will forever go on to eternity by saving souls and changing lives.

Galatians 1:3–4; Colossians 1:13–14; 2 Peter 1:2–4;

Beautiful One,

I notice all that you are doing and all that you are giving just to be close to Me. I notice all that you are giving to know Me. I notice you being attentive to the experience and seeing Me in everyone you meet. It is beautiful how attentive you are to all of your surroundings, experiencing Me and seeing them as messages from Me. You are beginning to understand that in everything I am all around you, giving you symbolic messages, mysterious whispers of how to enjoy and appreciate the day. Your attunement to My presence in this capacity is drawing you nearer to Me by softening and increasing your compassionate heart for others. I notice that in everything you do, you are looking to encounter Me. Keep seeking, keep noticing, and keep pressing forward in our intimate dance, and you are going to keep experiencing Me in new and supernatural ways. Pursuing Me with all your heart to encounter Me is growing an unshakable, immovable, and unstoppable faith and precious works in My name. Your foundation is solid, your heart is pure, your thoughts are set on Me, your eyes are focused, your deeds and works are intentional, and you are going to see abundance and a harvest like you have never earned or produced in your own strength. Once your next steps unfold, all is going to fall into place with the right people, the finances, and the resources in order to carry out our intentional work together to save souls and create healing. You are My obedient servant who will love all the clients that I send you to create a community of love for My kingdom. Love is what covers a multitude of things. We are all called to love. Beautiful One, you have found your soul's life purpose and mission. You have become one with Me in unity to find, hear, and know your calling. Continue to stay so close to Me that you lose sight of everything else around you. That is the key to fulfilling our vision and work together.

Matthew 7:24–27; 1 Corinthians 13:4–7

Beautiful One,

On this morning know that because My Son, Jesus Christ, overcame death, you too have overcome all of your battles and struggles in My name. When you fully trust and believe in only Me, you will have peace and know that I have already overcome as well in My strength. You don't have to understand, strive, or control things to work out; just come and rest in My presence, and watch Me mysteriously unfold answers to your prayers. They are already manifesting even though you can't clearly see it right now. Be patient, rest, and give Me praise for what is to come with expectancy. I delight in you in all your ways, so I ask that you too delight in Me even when you feel alone and can't see or hear Me. Draw nearer to Me, and I will show you why this has been necessary and how it all is going to unfold. My plans are to prosper you, but you must have an unshakable faith in all unknowns and circumstances. This is strengthening your faith. Have faith and hope for what is to come, even though you can't see it yet. I want to fulfill and answer My children's prayers, but it must be all in My divine timing and My way because I work all things out for your good. Keep trusting and believing because a harvest is on its way, a harvest that you could not produce or even imagine possible. Your heart is pure, compassionate, and selfless. I see all of that and know that you are committed to serving Me and My lost children and saving souls. You have many gifts and talents, Beautiful One, and that's why I chose you to be a warrior and vessel of My love and truth to lead all that you meet to Me so that they can have eternal life. The warmth, love, compassion, and light that radiate naturally from you will inherently draw others to you. Just watch how I bring people and resources to you. Simply trust and rest in My promises and truth.

Psalm 67:6; 85:12; 2 Corinthians 9:10

July 7

Beautiful One,

More and more people who want to be a part of this ministry are going to overflow to you. I will send the right people, but always listen for My affirmation of whether they are a good fit to embrace and live this mission with the intent of "being a servant to build a community of love." Have no fears or worries. It's all going to come abundantly and effortlessly, growing and increasing in your place in a very short period. Continue to spend time with Me in prayer and meditation, giving Me first priority above all else. When you are fully in tune with Me, the enemy can't touch you, and you can easily discern My voice and block him out. As you are in constant prayer and meditation with Me, you can't go wrong, and I will not let you fail. Beautiful One, we are going to do great things and save many souls.

Proverbs 19:17; 28:27; 1 Thessalonians 5:11

Beautiful One,

You are grateful, and I see and know that as I look upon your heart. There are sometimes instances, though, when your ego tries to become overbearing. It's not a lot, but it is enough that if I don't reveal it to you, you will fall back into the same cycle of bondage that controlled your life before. Be aware of constantly evaluating yourself, your actions, your motives, and your choices. Discern where it is coming from. Is it My still, small voice, or is it your overbearing ego wanting to be noticed? Your heart is pure, and you know your calling and your soul's life purpose. Continue to come to Me each day, wrestling with your thoughts and questions of what you are supposed to do. This will keep you in balance, at peace, and one with Me, allowing Me to direct your each and every step. This will prevent you from diverging off My path for you. This is important because if any wrong steps are taken, time is lost for our intentional work together. We are so close to beginning an amazing work together, so I want you to stay so close to Me that you lose sight of everything else that you see. I'm so glad you paid attention to your bodily felt sense, because I was able to reveal this message to you.

Ecclesiastes 3:1–8

Beautiful One,

Do you now understand why the fiery darts are so fierce toward you? You are My chosen one for spiritual warfare. You are going to be leading others to Me and saving souls. I have seen how you have been targeted and attacked, but continue to rebuke the enemy because I already have won this battle for you. Keep pressing in toward Me and through this. The time is near that all of this is going to unfold quickly. I will show you how. Trust and believe that I have this all worked out in My timing. I only ask that you rest, pray, meditate, and praise Me for all that I have already done. I knew I could rely on you. You have a soft, warm, compassionate heart, but also one ready to stand against any foe for a greater cause than yourself. Thank you for your obedience, discipline, and love for Me. I know that I can rely solely on you to lead this mission. I will keep surrounding you with the right people with the right resources. Finances are not going to be an issue either. There will be someone who will come forward and ask if they can provide resources to you to get this started. It is close, Beautiful One. Trust and believe in Me, and keep doing the next thing I put before you.

Zechariah 3:2; Hebrews 12:2; James 4:7

Beautiful One,

You already have everything that you need for this day and each day. I go before you, with you, and behind you. All I ask is that you trust and believe that My Word and promises are true. You are letting the enemy distract you with anxious thoughts and feelings. Come to Me when you notice this so that I can increase your faith and steadfastness. This testing is increasing the wisdom and faith that you need to be solely dependent upon Me. I am the one who gives you rest, peace, wisdom, and abundance. Nothing of this world can fill your desires. They may temporarily, but I assure you, they are impermanent and will leave you empty and walking spiritually dead. That is not what I have planned for you. As I have told you, you are My chosen one whom I have called to be My frontline warrior to save souls. The enemy's attacks are fierce because He knows your heart, determination, courage, and discipline. The enemy sees that you are willing to lose yourself in order to gain your full potential that I have called you to walk out for My purpose and will in My kingdom. Everyone has a calling and purpose that I have impregnated within them before they were conceived. However, only a few heed the calling seriously and decide to actively live out the calling by faith. Beautiful One, I know how difficult it is to feel like you are on this journey alone, carrying out your calling for My purpose. I assure you that this feeling too will pass as you become stronger and steadfast in My Word, truth, and promises. Just be on guard that the enemy is trying to torment you during this part of the journey because he knows how close you are to a major breakthrough. I promise you, Beautiful One, your harvest is near, and you will then see the way. All your efforts, tears, pain, and sacrifices are worth what I have prepared for you. It is up to you whether you elect to see what I have prepared for you. I can promise you that it is greater than anything you have planned. My thoughts, plans, desires, sight, hearing, love, and peace are ones that you can't ever begin to imagine. Let Me take you to the center of My heart so that you can experience all of My supernatural powers and gifts here so that you can experience where heaven meets earth in a new dimension. It is at this place that you will be equipped to serve and minister to a mass of people. You will not believe your eyes, and you will know that it is all from Me. That is what I have and want for you, Beautiful One. Stay so close to Me, and give Me fully your heart. Surrender all of your heart. Every part of your heart needs to be given to Me so that our hearts are as one in union. This will be a direct connection to My thoughts, My words, and My feelings that will give you the gift of prophecy to speak over others what I need to reveal to them. This is My only opportunity to touch or speak into some of these people's lives because they don't know how to be still, pray, and meditate in My presence. They are unable or unwilling to make space to hear from Me. That is where I will use you to speak My words, truth, promises, and love into them. Do you understand now why I need all of you? I need all of your heart—fully!

Exodus 13:21; Deuteronomy 31:8; Isaiah 45:2

Beautiful One,

I see your heart and need for Me. As you continue to bow down to My feet, you relinquish more of yourself and your ways to Me. It is here that you find My rest. Without Me your plans and day fall apart. Let Me guide your heart and your day will go effortlessly. Continue to come to Me for all your plans, needs, and desires each and every hour. None are too small or too big for Me. I want to provide and sustain you. I am your only defense so that you can have righteousness. I love it when you depend upon Me and need Me. That is when the veil can be removed and I do the most work within you. Continue to seek Me and need Me. I am doing a new thing in you that is significant. Beautiful One, I see how grateful you are. Continue to praise Me and be grateful in all you do. A heart of gratitude shows your need for Me. It crushes and diminishes the enemy's power over you. I am working all things in your life for your greater good. Through Christ I meet all of your needs before you even know what they may be.

Psalm 62:1–2; 73:26; 136:16

Beautiful One,

As you start your day with Me, I orchestrate your steps and divinely prepare the way for you. You are not alone, and I am walking with you on this journey. You will go forward, completing all your tasks and obligations in My name. As I have revealed to you your inner depths, I have revealed and unfolded who you are in Christ. Now that you have recklessly abandoned yourself, we have much work to do together, and your full potential and creativity will be unleashed. You are my beautiful child who will selflessly serve and bless others. You know your calling, you know your mission, you know your purpose and meaning, you know who you are in Christ, and you know to keep in My presence. Stay true to yourself and your higher divine inner self, and you will not waver, become distracted, or be shaken in your faith. You are now built upon the strong foundation of My truth, My light, and My words. Now you are equipped to send forth My light.

John 10:3; Romans 8:30; Jude 1:1

Beautiful One,

You have been called to send forth your light with grace. Come to Me for rest, and I will give you peace to sustain you. I am always with you, even when the waters get muddy. I will use it to nourish your soul. Release, relax, and let go, Beautiful One. As one door is closing, another one is opening. The old and the past no longer serves you, and opportunities are emerging. Trust and believe by being open to receive it. It is more than what you could expect or imagine. I have only the best for you and have been waiting for you to accept this closing door. You already have the answers already within you. Trust My Spirit's leading and guiding. Trust and believe that you are equipped with gifts and talents to live out your soul's life purpose and mission. Your walk will be an example to others to lead them to Me. Abundance is being manifested into your life. You are walking in your true calling, and I am well pleased with you, Beautiful One.

Ephesians 4:1; Philippians 3:14; 2 Thessalonians 1:11

July 14

Beautiful One,

Give your anxious feelings and internal jitters to Me. These are a result of fear. Trust and believe that I am meeting all of your needs before you even know what they are. Focus on Me and the divine inner spark within. I am manifesting your heart's desires even though you don't see anything happening. Don't resist the healing and transformation that are taking place. Your resistance is delaying My truth and inhibits your progress of where I am taking you. Let go of your dark thoughts and embrace the process. Be patient with yourself and open to My loving correction. You will one day understand, and blessings will come forth. Let me awaken your soul. Let Me awaken your soul.

Isaiah 60:1; Galatians 2:20; Ephesians 5:14

Beautiful One,

I am equipping you to be a spiritual healer to inspire others. I have chosen you because of your courage and ability to go to deep dark places. Divine energy, creativity and perseverance go with you. You meet others with much love and nonjudgment in their most desperate times. You believe that there is good in everyone, no matter what they have done, where they have been, or where they currently are, and that is a balm. You are My vessel where earth meets heaven. Remember, you are not traveling alone. I am always with you, and I will surround you with others to come along with you, so embrace and accept the help. This is not for you to do alone. This is a community effort. These companions will nourish your soul and fill you up when you need rejuvenating. It is all part of My plan for you. Let it all unfold mysteriously and effortlessly in My timing.

Psalm 133:1; Romans 12:4–5; Hebrews 10:24–25

Beautiful One,

You hear and know My voice, and I am your comforter and strength in all things. My plans for you are great. I have chosen you because of your warm spirit, autonomy, and ability to manage this calling. You channel My love to everyone you meet, even when they are difficult. You have the capacity to take charge but do so humbly. You have so much love, compassion, and wisdom to share with others. I see your heart and desire to serve others selflessly. In all things, you offer unconditional positive care and warmth. I am inspired by your efforts, dedication, and faithfulness to serve Me. Your spirit will bring light to others.

Psalm 119:105 ; Matthew 5:14–16; John 8:12

July 17

Beautiful One,

I want to encompass you with My peace. As you travel with Me on this journey, I am with you every step of the way. It is exhilarating to show you My signs and wonders at each destination where you arrive. You are ascending to greater heights. This pilgrimage is life-changing and transformative. As we continue to these new depths and arrive at new pinnacle points, I will reveal more of My truth to you. I delight in giving you affirmations and unfolding your next steps. I am captivated by your wonder and reverence for Me as I surprise you with My mysterious ways. Nothing can separate you from the love that I have for you, Beautiful One.

John 9:5; Ephesians 5:7–14; Colossians 1:9–14

Beautiful One,

Do you know that there is nothing you have to do to prepare for this journey? I only ask you to come with expectancy to encounter Me in ways that you have never experienced before. I want My words and promises to come alive to you as you meditate more on My Word in My presence. My Word is an expression of My feelings that I have toward you. Let My Word be an inspiration to you in how to live each day fully. As you grow deeper in My Word, it increases your spiritual awareness and releases your creativity that I impregnated you with. As you mature into your gifts that I have equipped you with, you will go out and share them others. Beautiful One, you are right where you are supposed to be. Trust Me for the unfolding of this ministry, knowing that you will be fully equipped to go out in My name.

Daniel 2:22; Micah 6:8; 1 Corinthians 2:10

Beautiful One,

Be still, be still, be still, and know that I am God. Give Me your anxious thoughts and ways. I am doing a new thing in you, so surrender and let go. You can't even begin to see, hear, or understand what I am doing, but I am working and moving in your midst. I am working and moving in your midst. I am the light and truth. I am pouring that into you so that you can be My vessel to speak into others' lives who don't know Me or have a relationship with Me. Rest for a while and lie at My feet while I do this new thing in you. There is nothing you have to do or need to do, but just "be." Be with Me in My presence. I will give you peace, joy, affirmation, answered prayers, and the next steps you are seeking. Just be so that I can fill you fully and completely to prepare you for this next new thing. It is close, Beautiful one. Cling to My robe, and I won't let you fall. We have beautiful work and an amazing journey planned.

Exodus 14:14; Psalm 37:7; Habakkuk 2:20; Galatians 5:1

July 20

Beautiful One,

Just as My Son, Jesus Christ, and the disciples experienced spiritual warfare, I too have seen your attacks. Do as Jesus did, and pray for yourself and live out My truth and Word. As you pray and work in this world, just love all whom you meet and interact with, creating unity with one another in spirit and truth. Oftentimes spiritual conflict goes back many generations. Stand in the gap and pray for all, regardless of their journey, faith, culture, or background. Everyone is your brother or sister in Christ. Listen to hear their narratives in order to gain understanding of them personally so that they feel heard and affirmed, nurturing them with unconditional love. The love that you share with others may be the first time they have ever experienced such love. Let them see, feel, and know Me in all of your interactions, offering them hope. Love covers all, endures all, and is the greatest act of kindness that we can give freely to our brothers and sisters in hope of creating unity and peace just as Jesus gave. It begins with you; then it becomes contagious and multiplies. This is how we defeat the enemy.

Psalm 133:1; 1 Corinthians 13:7; 1 Timothy 2:1

Beautiful One,

Peace be within you. Extend your hand toward Mine and firmly grip My hand. Feel My loving presence around you like a gentle wind that is My breath. Breathe in deeply more of Me. The deeper you inhale, the more you experience Me. I am filling you from the inside out with My peace, joy, grace, mercy, protection, and unending love. I am clothing you with compassion, kindness, humility, gentleness, and kindness. This will allow you to forgive your grievances just as I have forgiven you. Let the peace of Christ fill you and rule in your heart. We are all interconnected and bound together, so whatever you send out is what you will receive in return. Above all, love is the greatest of these and binds us all together in perfect unity.

Colossians 3:12–17

Beautiful One,

I want you to know and feel that I do dwell within you. That is where your strength and power come from. Call upon Me in the time of adversity. You are rooted in My love, but you have no earthly conceptualization of how wide and long, how high and deep My love is for you. This is what I want you to experience so that I can fill you with My fullness. Beautiful One, if you allow Me, I will take you to the center of My heart, and you will be able to experience this fullness. You will then be a testimony to others of how they too can experience My fullness.

Ephesians 3:14–21

Beautiful One,

Your thoughts and focus are wandering from Me. Continue to remind yourself to stay so close to Me that you lose sight of everything else around you. Don't let the enemy distract you by leading you off to anxious thoughts and ways. The enemy wants you to wander from the narrow path that I have you on. Those anxious thoughts, jittery feelings, and trembling inside are not of Me. Pay attention to that and come to Me with these body-felt sensations and thoughts. When you are completely attuned to Me, the enemy has no power over you because I have already won this battle for you. Don't allow or give him any foothold or entry. You must trust and believe in My process and way for you. Put on your full body of armor of protection. Maintain your faith, hope, and love. The greatest of all of these is love. Love will protect you, and it perseveres. Love will not fail you. Sit back, rest, and relax in My presence, and watch what I am doing in your life. I am doing a new thing, but you must learn to "be" in My presence and let go of control. Surrender to My ways so that there are no obstacles and I can freely work in and through you. I want to show you everything that I have for you, Beautiful One. It is more than you could ever plan or imagine. Let Me unfold the mysteries of My ways so that I can show you My glory. You will be a testimony to the masses of what I did in your life. Let go, let go, let go, and let *Me*—I have more for you!

Genesis 24:12–14; 1 Corinthians 13

Beautiful One,

I am preparing you for a journey that you are not expecting. I ask that you wait patiently upon Me. Wait with hope and be still, and I will reveal to you My work in you. In your weakness and not knowing what to pray for anymore, that is okay because the Spirit intercedes on your behalf. I predestined you with a specific meaning, purpose, and life mission for My kingdom. This journey is also predestined for this appointed time. Have hope that I am going to reveal Myself to you in profound ways. Be hopeful and expectant, seeking to encounter Me. Just know that I am securely holding you in My arms, protecting you. If I am for you, who can be against you? Trust and believe.

Romans 8:26–30

July 25

Beautiful One,

I know this journey seems daunting at times, like you are walking alone in a narrow alley unsure of where you are headed. Continue on and do not be distracted by obstacles or worldly desires that may take you off this narrow alley. I know the steps seem difficult to ascend at times, but you are getting closer to your destination. It is okay to stop and rest when you feel weary. Rest in My presence when you need it. This will invigorate you for the continued journey. I hope you are sensing our deep connection.

Psalm 54:4; Isaiah 41:10; Matthew 28:20

Beautiful One,

Something is shifting and happening within you. You can sense it, but you are unsure how to understand it. I am breathing down upon you. I am really close and near to you. You sense it because you are trembling and weeping. I am doing something new within you that is for the greater good. It is a plan to prosper you and not harm you. Meditate and gaze into My presence. Keep your focus on Me. The vision that you are getting of a royal person in a purple robe is of Me. I am holding a fountain pen with a sharp arrow point with intense red ink. I am writing a new song and narrative upon your heart. This etching will be painful at first, but it comes with much beauty. You cannot see what I wrote yet because you are not ready for it. You must continue to grow in your relationship with Me, which will help you grow into the new song and narrative that I have placed upon your heart.

Genesis 32:28; Isaiah 62:2; Acts 8:26

July 27

Beautiful One,

I am your shepherd, and you are My sheep. What that means is that I lead and you follow Me. This is new for you because you have always done things your own way with your own plans, seeking your own desires. For the past several years, I have been chasing after you, My lost sheep, trying to reveal to you My greater plan and will for your life. I have been so patient, loving, gentle, kind, and sometimes piercing while trying to get your attention. My message is still the same: let go, give up control, and sit in the ambiguity as I continue to hollow you out as an empty vessel so that there are no obstacles or distractions. I have great plans for you. I know this work of recklessly abandoning yourself has been painful and exhausting. You have been resistant and rebellious, trying to negotiate with Me your desires and My will. It doesn't work that way. When you say yes to the calling, you must die each and every day by letting go of all worldly desires that you try to cling to. These things that you cling to are impermanent. I want you to experience all of Me by living out your full potential of who I created you to be.

Isaiah 40:11; John 10:11; 1 Peter 5:4

Beautiful One,

Come to Me and sit at My feet. I know you are seeking answers of confirmation and asking what your next steps are. I know it seems that the next steps are big, and I sense your fear and doubt. You want to know for sure if you are on the right path, moving in the right direction. Trust in My leading and guiding. Trust also that if you do take a wrong step, the door will not open, and you will be directed back to where you are supposed to be. Part of your fear is that if you move forward, it closes the door to the past, which goes against your fleshly desires. I know you question whether or not I hear you. I do hear you. I am here with you. I am patiently waiting on you to see what choice you will make. Either choice will be painful. The first is to move forward by putting the past behind you. That will be painful. The second is as you move on, it too will be painful because it will be something new that takes you out of your comfort zone. Just trust the next step and know that My grace is sufficient. My grace abounds and will carry you through.

Joshua 1:9; Jeremiah 29:11–14; Philippians 1:2

Beautiful One,

I want nothing more than for you to have joy, to be carefree, and to have faith like a little child. You are a mighty warrior. Remember that it is no longer what others have done to you, but what I have done to see you through. I know you have experienced much crisis, trauma, pain, and heartbreak in your lifetime. I am going to use it all for My ministry. Your trust in Me has strengthened your faith. You have channeled your pain to one of compassion for all instead of falling prey to being a victim by placing blame. You are going to serve as an example to others, guiding them to Me. Your narrative will be a testimony of how I transformed your pain into great beauty with intentional purpose and meaning. I am leading and directing all of your next steps. Trust and believe in Me to lead, guide, and direct the way.

Matthew 18:2–4; Mark 10:13–16; Luke 18:17

Beautiful One,

I am calling you to be an example of how to live just as Jesus lived when under the occupation of the Romans. Jesus was tempted, waited for answered prayers, and was oppressed, mocked, and even denied. No matter what you may be going through, continue to follow Jesus. I know that great divide and conflict arise from the various interpretations of My Word, so approach each situation with prayer and discernment. I am calling you to be all-inclusive with others, sharing in faith and love for all with Me at the center of all interactions. This is how peace and justice will be ultimately achieved. Jesus walked and lived each day on this pathway. It begins with you having an open heart and open mind, allowing Me to lead the process. Then put your faith into action by speaking up and supporting those who are marginalized. This all must be done with peace, nonviolence, and love for all. This is how you create unity and end such injustices. Remember, "Blessed are the peacemakers."

John 13:13–16; 1 Corinthians 11:1; Ephesians 5:1–2

Beautiful One,

I am with you. I've always been with you. I will not leave or forsake you. I am strengthening your faith and moving in your midst even though you can't see or comprehend what I am doing. Dear child, My plans are good for you. I do see your heart, and I have counted your tears. Things will work out as I have divinely orchestrated for you. You will not be disappointed, but will glorify Me for what I have done in your life. Continue to be still with Me, waiting and listening for your next steps. This is not your vision to carry and bring to fruition, but mine so that I can show you My glory and how I work all things according to My timing for the good of those who love Me. I see your faith, your love, and your discipline. Trust and believe, Beautiful One. Your harvest is near. We have much work to do together. Let Me show you how. Surrender and let go so that I can show you how.

Habakkuk 3:4; Matthew 17:5; Revelation 19:1

Beautiful One,

I am the beginning and the end. I have begun good and new works in you, and I will finish them to completion. I know you weep for the loss of your closest friends, family, and previous way of being. I know in this calling you sometimes feel like a prisoner. The night before Jesus' crucifixion, He spent the night in a prison cave, feeling alone and abandoned with no way of escape. Just as you grieve, Jesus too grieved. I know this seems like a really dark place to you, but I am with you in all of it, and I will not forsake you. I see your challenges and inner conflict between spirit and flesh. It will get easier, as I am strengthening your faith and moving in your midst. Jesus' best friend, Peter, also struggled with his faith and shortcomings, but it was with Peter that I built My church. I am working and doing the same with you. Be encouraged; it all is working out just as I have ordained in My perfect timing.

Psalm 88:8–9, 18; Isaiah 46:10; Revelation 22:13

Beautiful One,

I am awakening your soul that has been dormant for so long, that has been longing to be in My presence and perfect will. I am bringing forth your unconscious to the light, which I know takes much hard work, persistence, and determination. This phase is bringing forth positive life changes and opportunities. I am encouraging you to set things in motion to move forth in faith and trust that you are on the right path. I will lead your steps to help you achieve the vision that I have placed upon your heart. By following My lead and nudges, you will meet with success and fulfillment of your soul's life purpose and mission. I am your inspirational guiding light that will bring illumination to others to help them see their full potential and increase their spiritual awareness. There is so much healing energy that is coming forth.

Romans 1:19–23; 7:7–13

August 3

Beautiful One,

I see your weariness and thirst for peace and rest. Remember who you are and that you can do all things in Christ who strengthens you. Repeat that, and come to Me for sustenance and rest. As you do, you will become invigorated and stronger. I know the road often seems narrow and rough with steep inclines, slopes, and scary cliffs, but as you pick up your gait and walk boldly where I am leading you, enjoy the journey and majestic views. Keep your focus on Me, seeing Me in every detail of your life. Your experience in the wilderness and desert is only temporary, I assure you. Keep walking in faith.

Psalm 33:18–19; 54:4; 1 Philippians 4:13

Beautiful One,

Why do you continue to resist your calling? You know the vision and plan that I have for you, but you continue to question and doubt. Do you not trust and believe My plans for you? Let Me transfigure you into the person that I intended you to be and the work that I have ordained for you to do in My name for My kingdom. Let go of your thoughts, plans, desires, and wishes. Come and follow Me. I will lead you and show you how. My plans are greater than your plans. Trust and believe in My way and timing. Your heart's desire will be met and will be greater than you could ever plan or imagine for yourself. Stop resisting. Let Me show you My glory.

Matthew 17:1–13; Luke 9:28–36

Beautiful One,

I know you question what it means to be alive and joyful. I know you feel as though you are only going through the motions of the day without a plan or any order. I know this path seems lonely for you, and I understand your resistance to this calling. It is an internal conflict between your flesh and spirit that is causing you to feel anxious and sick. Continue to keep pressing forward courageously as I lead and nudge you, even though you can't see what I am doing. I know your pain and struggles feel like a thorn in your side that has been with you for years. This is a part of the transfiguring process that is piercing and purging all of your past infected wounds that you have repressed. I will heal all of your wounds, leaving a scar so that you will be reminded where you have been, what you have endured, and how I am going to use your wounds to heal others. No matter what the situation is, you will be able to sit and be with others with great empathy and compassion. It is your personal pain that awakens your soul, making you feel most fully alive, especially when you can look into others' eyes and resonate with their pain. There is no greater expression of love than when you can enter into others' pain by being fully present with them, affirming their experience. This is what it means to be fully alive in Christ: when you use your personal experiences to put your faith into action to selflessly serve those who are also suffering. Because My Son was able, you too are able to serve in this capacity.

Luke 1:38; Ephesians 2

Beautiful One,

    Through your confession of sins and repentance, you brought light to your darkness, which released the stronghold of the enemy upon you. Your past choices caused you much suffering and pain. Even though Jesus was without sin, He too suffered great pain. Just know that I do not give you more than you can handle. Be thankful for everything in your life that you have been able to experience, even your losses. When you interact with others who have hurt or deceived you, pray over them and love them. That is a deep, sincere gift that you can give to others that goes beyond your own strength. There is no better way to show Jesus' love.

2 Chronicles 7:14; Psalm 32:5; Acts 3:19

Beautiful One,

My Spirit blows around you like a steady wind with power to shift and move things on your behalf. You can't see or understand completely what I am doing other than just knowing that something is shifting within you. The shifting can be intense, but My transformative grace abounds in you, making it all bearable to withstand. I have something so much greater for you than your plans. Mary had no idea that she was going to give birth to a Savior. I too am birthing something significant within you. Just as Mary was courageous to say yes to live out her divine calling, you too are courageous and can follow in her footsteps. Continue to trust and believe, knowing that I do not give you more than you can handle because with Me all things are possible. Trust Me—you don't want to miss what I have planned for you.

Amos 4:13; Luke 1:38; John 3:8

August 8

Beautiful One,

As the sun rises over the skyline, the radiating light awakens the dawn with infinite possibilities within the day. Reflect and stay in My radiating presence. It is My presence that gives you peace, calm, and discernment for your day. Walk courageously in My strength, but also with gentleness and kindness, exalting My name. Just as the ocean's waves ebb and flow, so will your day as long as you are fully in My presence. As things unfold for you in an effortless manner, you will experience great joy and excitement from within that can't be fulfilled with anything from this world. I give you My peace here on earth as it is in heaven, but you must be fully in My presence.

Job 42:2; Jeremiah 32:17; Mark 14:36

Beautiful One,

You are like a buoy, and I am the living water that flows in, through, and all around you. No matter the storms, winds, or intense heat that you may go through, I will sustain you and not let you go. You are anchored in My presence. Just as a buoy is free floating, so too will you be free floating, going along with the waves that are nudging and moving you to where I want you to be. In the middle of the storm, there is no need to feel scared, because I am in control and your security rests in Me. You will not be overcome by the waters or the storms.

Isaiah 43:2; Colossians 2:5; Hebrews 6:19

August 10

Beautiful One,

I have seen your mourning with regard to this calling that I have placed upon you. I am asking you to embrace this calling instead of resisting it. Let Me mold and transform you into who I intended you to be so that I can reveal Myself to you in supernatural ways. It is at this place where you will experience Me fully with joy overflowing. Walk into it, leaving all doubts behind you. This vision is greater than you, so abandon your narrow-minded thinking and selfish desires, which are impermanent. Rely solely on My Spirit to guide you, and release all flesh and worldly distractions. No longer are you doing this alone, because I am sending others to you who will embrace this ministry to fruition. It is a ministry building a community of love, not self-seeking recognition. It is about the unseen opportunities that your limited sight can't recognize. It is about being open to the Spirit's leading and not your preconceived plans. It is about your life speaking through Jesus Christ so that all can see His light, truths, promises, and eternal glory of where heaven meets earth. Receive this gift, and then share it by giving it away.

Isaiah 41:25; 64:8; 2 Corinthians 4:7

August 11

Beautiful One,

When you pray, pray boldly and courageously in My name for everything that I have ordained for you. Your prayers I hear, but they are too small and narrow-minded. Pray to let it be My will to be done here on earth as it is in heaven. I will rain down on you boldly much more than what you could imagine or expect. This is how I want to show you My glory. Pray boldly and courageously.

Hebrews 4:16; James 5:16; 1 John 5:14–15

Beautiful One,

The enemy's attacks are fierce toward you, but also toward your family, which directly affects you. I have given you the strength and courage of a lion to take command and authority over this situation. Enter into your intercessory prayer stance by sweeping your family's house by anointing them for protection and deliverance from the enemy's stronghold. You are an overcomer and can face the enemy boldly to cast off the constant conflict and turmoil. Defend your family, and use the authority that I have given to you in the name of My Son, Jesus Christ. A breakthrough is about to take place that will not only free all the strongholds on your family, but also release you to walk into the new phase of your journey. Don't delay.

Romans 8:38; Ephesians 1:19–22; Colossians 2:10

Beautiful One,

As you reach out your hand to Me, you feel the vibrations of My strength and energy flowing through you. This is not my full My power. You are not capable of receiving My full power. I sense your frustration of where you are right now. You are frustrated that you don't know or see My full plans for you. Rest assured, I am working and weaving the right people into your life behind the scenes to help fulfill the vision and your destiny for My kingdom. Your frustration is temporary, and My plan and order are indefinite; however that takes precedence over anything that you are feeling or experiencing right now. You will see, know, and experience My glory when the time is right. I'm going to use the frustration that has worn you down paper thin, making you transparent. This is the place where I can use you even more and build you up to what you were supposed to do and be prior to life circumstances and influences altering your path. Stop resisting, Beautiful One, so that this transformation can proceed, removing obstacles, because we have a lot of work to accomplish. Release your thoughts, feelings, and emotions to Me. I want you to experience everything that I have prepared for you. The question is, do you?

Matthew 16:15–19; Luke 9:1; 10:19

August 14

Beautiful One,

You are experiencing an increase in your life with accelerated progress. Continue to be persistent and joyful in each and every small detail that I put before you. Blessings evolve from gratitude, and what you have sown you shall now reap. This is a time of seeing a harvest of blessings that will not only multiply to you, but overflow into others. I have noticed the sacrifices you have made and your willingness to give yourself unconditionally to others. Your giving and encouraging attitude illuminates My light from you into others. Continue on this path that illuminates My light.

Leviticus 26:5; Matthew 9:37; 2 Corinthians 9:10

Beautiful One,

Just as the ocean's waves ebb and flow, so too does life. Each day is a new day, so remember to journal what I reveal to you each day so that you can see My hand in every circumstance. I give you affirmations and visions each day that I don't want you to miss. This creates enthusiasm within you, confirming My plans for you and eliminating doubts and fears. It is My enthusiasm that encompasses you that is My divine strength. I am empowering you to do what you were intended and created to do. All of your skills and talents I am going to use to the fullest. It is all connected to what I have been doing in you. Deep passion, enjoyment, and energy are welling up inside of you with vibrations that exude from you, revealing your potential and creativity. With Me in you and you in Me, there is nothing that we can't do. Keep pressing in closer and walking out each step where I direct you. Even though these may seem like big steps, you will have peace and comfort in all of this. Yes, I know it seems crazy, but don't worry or be scared about what others may say or how they treat you. I have showed you that I am in control, and I am carrying you each step of the way. Remember that you can do all things through Me who strengthens you, but you are also everything that I am because I dwell within you. You have limitless ability if you possess it and use it.

Psalm 28:7; 32:8; 118:24

August 16

Beautiful One,

As you continue to affirm your commitment to My plans for you and release more and more of the past, your pain, your desires, and your plans to My way, the enemy will make fierce attacks upon you. Surround yourself with prayer partners for protection. Call out to Me, letting Me know how you are feeling and what you are experiencing. That is what intimate friends do for each other, and I want to hear and know everything you are feeling and experiencing. Rely solely upon Me. Hold on to the enthusiasm that I give you, and keep repeating that you won't be shaken or deterred about where I am leading you because I am with you. Stay so close to Me that you lose sight of everything that you see.

Numbers 6:24–25; 1 Corinthians 10:13; 2 Corinthians 10:4–5

August 17

Beautiful One,

Your stomach is in knots, and it is nervousness. Let Me untie the knots, and let Me show you how. The nervousness is because you are moving on and putting the past behind you. You are feeling threatened, controlled, and manipulated by others who are causing fear within you. Rebuke this, and don't allow them to have this type of control over you, preventing you from achieving the ministry that I have placed on your heart. I am so glad that you are seeking Me during this time because I can take these knots and turn them into much beauty and potential within you.

Isaiah 61:1–3; Matthew 18:18; Hebrews 5:7

Beautiful One,

Sometimes when you feel uncontrollable trembling and internal sickness, it is the groaning of your soul that I am allowing. The soul's groaning is a way to loosen the strongholds on your inner depths and release both conscious and unconscious thoughts that you may not be aware of. The vibrations release but also restore energy, new growth, and potential that is within you. I know it is a scary, dark, cold, and difficult place to be, but it is one that is necessary. Face these times with courage, discipline, and stamina by sitting through them instead of trying to avoid them by sidestepping My process. Don't reach out for temporary or impermanent worldly things, trying to fill this with short-term pleasures. These things won't last and will never fulfill you the way that I can. My love is all-encompassing and breaks through to your deepest inner being during this groaning process, creating healing.

Matthew 9:28–30; Romans 8:26–27; 2 Corinthians 10:4

August 19

Beautiful One,

I have been singing and rejoicing over you all night. I knew you would get to this place in your weakness, revealing you have nothing to give and are unable to begin this ministry. That is where I needed you so that I could show you My glory of what I am doing in My strength and power and not yours. The things that you normally depend on — finances, relationships, possessions, and yourself — have been depleted and stripped from you so that you will seek Me more and wait upon Me so I can show you My glory, Beautiful One. I want to show you how I will unfold all of this before you with nothing for you to bring or give but just your willing, surrendered heart.

Psalm 138:3; Isaiah 40:29; 2 Corinthians 12:10

Beautiful One,

I know this was one of your hardest days yet with fierce enemy attacks. Know that you are on the right path, or you would not be getting such fierce attacks. I know you feel like giving up. You wonder when the hurt will stop, and you question when I will intervene and move you forward, when doors will open, when your hardship will end, when I will show you My glory and work at hand, and many, many more "when, when, when" questions. I know you said you can't go any lower and can't hold on any longer like this. That is right. You can't continue to hold onto all of your personal desires and outcomes. Let go! Let go! I will reach out and catch you. Let go and surrender even more, Beautiful One. I want to carry you and give you rest and peace. A long-awaited change is about to take place.

Psalm 35

August 21

Beautiful One,

You have endured much this week. Come to Me for rest and
meditation to let My grace and love fall upon you like a gentle
shower of rain. It's a warm day, but there is a cool shower to
comfort you and give you peace. Be still and just relax in My
presence to let Me nourish you this day. It is My living water that
will put new life in you, allowing your beauty and potential to grow
to heights you never knew or experienced before. I will renew your
energy and give you more time in this day that only I can give.

Psalm 61:1; Proverbs 19:23; Jeremiah 31:25

Beautiful One,

Pay attention to your body-felt sense and when I awaken you in the middle of the night. I have special instructions that I must relay to you just like a watchman on the outlook. I need you to be intentional with spending quiet time with Me during this time because I will be giving you specific instructions of your next steps. As you encounter difficulties or other people, it is important to handle them with care, loving-kindness, and patience. This allows My divine energy to positively flow so that there will be no interruption of My abundant blessings that will manifest success in all you do. This is a daily practice of denying yourself and surrendering your day, order, and self to Me. I am all about order, and it has to be My order. When you acknowledge Me first, I will direct your steps and not lead you astray.

Psalm 127:1; 130:6; Isaiah 27:3; 58:8

Beautiful One,

I reveal Myself to you in many different ways and symbols. Pay attention to your surroundings and see what in nature may speak to you. Spend time with it and see if it is revealing a message to you. There is interconnectedness with all of My creation. Nature goes through a metaphorical process as a seed being placed, nourished, birthed, grown, then death. You are no different. Your life is a birthing process that ebbs and flows with the changing of the seasons. This awakens your soul if you say yes to this process to allow it to happen effortlessly. It gives you greater clarity, wisdom, and a vision for things that never seemed possible. I am growing your spiritual sight, purifying your heart, and clearing your thoughts to be like Mine. You are victorious. Where there is victory, much opportunity and advantage exist.

John 3:3; 2 Corinthians 5:7; Hebrews 11:6

Beautiful One,

You continue to do the next steps that I put before you. That is what I want you to do. This is a time of developing your patience and seeing if you will do each radical thing that I place upon your heart. I know you have others questioning you and saying things to you that you are being irrational and crazy. I say to you that you are being obedient and faithful with what I continue to place upon your heart. It delights Me that you are trusting Me even though you are being scrutinized by others. Your discipline and obedience to Me will be rewarded, and others will see how I use you. This will reveal My glory, and they no longer will say or believe that you are irrational or crazy. Continue to be quiet with Me and let Me whisper to you your next steps. Part of your work is also to be on guard that inferior thoughts do not influence you. When they do, call upon Me and I will take them.

Psalm 40:1–3; Psalm 112:6–8; Luke 17:5

Beautiful One,

Because of your faith and God-led decisions, I know you have been called irrational and crazy. It is called living radically each day for Me by taking up My cross and recklessly abandoning yourself. This is how you know you are on the right path when others call you these things because this is not the normal way of the world. I see your sacrifices and willingness to surrender all to know Me more. Continue stepping out of your comfort zone, and I will show you more of who I am. I am thankful you have decided not to settle for the superficial things of this world, but more of My supernatural abundance that only I can give. Be still during this time. Listen for My voice, and you will see how I am moving to mine your inner depths like a gemstone ready to be polished and revealed.

Daniel 11:35; 12:10; Matthew 16:24–26; Luke 9:23

August 26

Beautiful One,

I hear your prayers of uncertainty of not knowing or hearing what your next steps are. I have seen your obedience, and you wonder why the next door has not opened. Give Me your restlessness, anxiousness, and sick feelings. I will take it all from you and give you rest and peace. You are missing what I am doing during this time of calming your driven, overbearing self. I am instructing you to take only small steps in My perfect timing. Remain focused, steadfast, but even more importantly, more dependent upon Me. The seeds have been planted within you, and I am nourishing those seeds so that they will bear much fruit. There is a great harvest that is coming in My perfect timing. Wait, and don't rush the process. Wait upon Me. There is a reason for My order. Trust and believe. I want to give you more than you can imagine. Wait with expectancy.

Psalm 19:1; 104:5–9

Beautiful One,

This process has been one of putting you on a firm foundation of My truth and promises. This new solid structure that I am rebuilding within you is placing you on the highest ground for all to see like a lighthouse. You will be like a lighthouse that is a beacon of light to others, helping them navigate the rough seas, the blinding fog, and the potential dangers surrounding them. A lighthouse does stand alone, as you often feel, but you are not alone because I am with you, overshadowing the light and the dark. Remember, I am the one who illuminates the light within you to be a beacon and focal point of strength and guidance and a spiritual safe harbor to all those who navigate toward you. Remember to keep your focus on Me when the waters seem rough and unbearable.

Matthew 5:16; John 8:12; Ephesians 5:7–14

Beautiful One,

In the waiting,
I am orchestrating order.
In the waiting,
I am cultivating your soul.
In the waiting,
I am giving you nourishment.
In the waiting,
You are learning submission.
In the waiting,
You are gaining perseverance.
In the waiting,
You are falling in love with Me.
In the waiting,
I will reveal My promises.
In the waiting,
There is a full reward.
In the waiting,
You are marked for My glory.
In the waiting,
You receive My authority.
In the waiting,
It is going to be more than you can imagine.

Wait, hope, and trust in Me!

Psalm 25:5; 27:14; Hosea 12:6

Beautiful One,

I see your restlessness and anxiousness. I am calling you to a time of stillness with Me because there are still some inferior elements within you that you need to recognize, acknowledge, and remove. Your overbearing ego is driving you to this place of restlessness and anxiousness. It wants you to push ahead in a careless and reckless manner, not knowing which foot goes on the gas and which foot goes on the brake. There is serious danger in this place. Restrain yourself by being quiet with Me, and continue to take small steps toward what I put before you. Be content with these small steps, knowing that this is creating balance, peace, and a steadfast progression that will result in this vision unfolding in its perfect timing effortlessly and successfully. Remain adaptable at this place and be tolerant of others, but remain detached from those with toxic influences. No action is required at this moment except for the tasks that I put before you that must be followed through with before I open the next door for you. Do not move ahead of Me, as this will result in disastrous results. Allow Me to use this time to continue to prepare you and others who will be coming alongside of you to make this vision come to fruition. Trust in Me. Accept the uncertainty at this moment, and sit in the ambiguity. Success is imminent, but it must be in My timing and My way.

Exodus 14:14; 1 Samuel 12:16; Zechariah 2:13

Beautiful One,

Allow Me to give order and direction for each and every thing you do. There is freedom in allowing Me to lead and guide you. By allowing Me to carry this all for you, your weight, burden, and yoke are light. When you do get tired, come to Me so that I can refill and refresh you with My living water. I yearn to be your all in each and every detail of your life. I will give you peace, strength, and contentment. I am shifting your desires, emotions, and pain by putting a new song in your heart. No longer will you mourn your losses because you will realize that all of this was part of My perfect plan to get you where you are today. You realize that others are not where you are on your spiritual journey, but I am working all things for the greater good in My perfect timing. Continue to put Me first in all your ways, even though you are experiencing resistance, scrutiny, and persecution. I will restore all your lost relationships to be more fruitful and loving than before. I know this journey to your inner depths has been painful, but I will reward you for all your effort and hard work. You are a special child to Me, and we have great work ahead of us.

Job 6:10; Psalm 34:18; Matthew 11:28–30

Beautiful One,

Continue to detach and remove yourself from inferior thoughts and situations. I know you have begun that work, but I ask you to search your heart, mind, and soul and release all of it to Me. This is an obstacle preventing your creative thoughts, feelings, and spirit to guide you. Once these are removed, your full potential will be released, and you will see My will be done for you. Get in touch with your inferior thoughts, and ask what it wants you to know about it so that you can acknowledge it and create unity with it. This will allow you to move on by releasing those negative, empty feelings and thoughts that have been a stronghold on you for far too long. Once this is released, your possibilities are limitless with potential. You will be free!

Matthew 19:26; Mark 10:27; Luke 18:27

September 1

Beautiful One,

You can't let the enemy enter your thoughts. He brings up the past and throws in images that are not as they appear. Stay mindful of the present moment of what is before you that you need to accomplish. That is how you stay closest to Me, and it deflects the enemy's fiery attacks. The enemy knows that you are near a major breakthrough, so he is using everything in his power to get to you. Stay so close to Me that you lose sight of his deceit and lies. I have overcome, and you are near to the next door of opportunity that I have for you. Press in, press through, and press forward. I am waiting there for you with open arms. This is a major door that will be the beginning of unfolding this ministry. Don't waver, but remain steadfast on the current path, Beautiful One.

Job 42:2; Jeremiah 32:17; John 15:4–5

September 2

Beautiful One,

You are right where you are supposed to be. Continue to listen and hear My voice. Don't let others distract or discourage you, because they are not where you are in a relationship with Me. You know My voice well, so don't doubt My plans or instructions for you. Continue what you are doing joyfully in My name. Proceed with balance and discipline by abandoning your personal desires and outcome. By saying yes to all the changes, hurt, pain, despair, loss of plans, and loss of relationships, you are fully trusting in My greater plans for you. You no longer are operating from your own selfish desires and plans, but you are coming into a higher consciousness by fully accepting My grace, mercy, and compassion to use you to unfold this ministry. All of this work is interconnected and working to refine your character so that you will be equipped to give unconditional love not only to others, but also to yourself, which thereby diminishes an overbearing ego. You are being redeemed, restored, and equipped to be My servant to all those that I send to you who are in despair, lost, or broken. I am giving you the capacity to hold darkness and light for yourself as well as others so that you can minister to them, breaking the stronghold that has continued to keep them stuck in this negative place of suffering and pain. Saying yes releases the control of the dark side, which will no longer evoke fear and anxiety within you. This will release your full potential and creativity.

Matthew 4:16; Luke 1:79; John 1:5

September 3

Beautiful One,

I am challenging you to look deeper into your inner depths. In order to do this, you must not look to the past nor look into the future, but stay in the midway point. The midway point will help you to stay present in the moment. Stay present in the moment with full abandonment and surrender so that I can show you My glory in how I am going to bring all of this together to fruition. Wait, wait patiently upon Me.

Psalm 113:4–6; 139:7–12

September 4

Beautiful One,

I have planted a seed into fertile soil. My Word is your nourishment that will sustain you. The more you grow in My Word and retain it, the stronger you become to stand against trials and adversity. My Word produces a crop for those who patiently endure and persevere. Listen carefully to how I speak to you through My Word. My Word brings light to the darkness of the things hidden and concealed. Take heart, though, from what you bring to the light; it will no longer control you. You will be released from the bondage of the enemy. You will be set free because even in the darkest depth, My light is enough. Nothing can keep the grace of My light from piercing through. Increase in My Word, which brings more light, and watch your seed sprout, producing a thriving harvest.

2 Timothy 3:16–17; Hebrews 4:12; James 1:22

Beautiful One,

As you are meditating, you are reflecting on the past and what went wrong. The work over the past several years has been to get you to see that in all of your past successes and achievements, you lacked having Me at the center of everything. This way was good for a time, but eventually you could no longer sustain this way of being. You became exhausted, depleted, and the sand beneath your feet began to crumble and give way. There was never a solid foundation under your feet to bless all of this. Now you are solely relying on Me and understand that only I am your rock and solid foundation. This is a process that may seem slow and hard to endure, but My way is necessary so that what is built upon this foundation will be an everlasting legacy honoring Me and My works, not yours. I know it seems to you like nothing is happening, but I promise you that mighty and great boulders are being set under your feet for the mighty and great works that will be transpiring from this place. Continue to be still and wait upon Me. You will know when My timing is perfect. Wait!

Proverbs 3:6; Matthew 6:33; Luke 12:29–31

Beautiful One,

An increase and an uprising are happening not only within you, but also around you, reaching out to all those who know you and see you. People are watching. You are My example, and others will be drawn to you, wondering what is different and how they too can experience your joy, even with everything you have endured. They don't know your real sorrow, but have sensed it and still see you praising Me. Just like an early dawn morning when the birds awaken with joyful praises and melodies, the roosters call out to a new day, and the cows moo with expectancy for their rations, you too will be joyful with praises, proclaiming a new day, and you will wait with expectancy for what I am doing and revealing to you. I see your restlessness in wanting to know more of Me and what I am causing to rise up within you. You sense and feel it to the point that you get no sleep, but you are rested. You fast, but are not hungry; you work tirelessly, but have more hours in the day; you meditate with Me, but want more and more. You can't get enough of knowing Me intimately and deeply. You are My chosen one, Beautiful One, the unlikely one just like Cyrus, who is going to lead and rebuild My kingdom. You are being called to be the watchman who will pray, hope, and save all people, not requiring rest, but you will be restless until you can begin this work and fulfill it. You have declared that you are Mine and I am yours. You have declared that you have given all of yourself to Me for My will to be done on earth as it is in heaven. I see your obedience, your discipline, and unconditional love for Me and others. Your heart is pure, and I have placed a new name upon your stone, revealing to you that you have overcome and the time is near for you to go and set forth your light like a lighthouse in a deep, dense fog around people who walk blindly in a daze. Set forth My truth and promises, saving My people.

Isaiah 45

Beautiful One,

All of the inner work that I am doing in you is near completion. All of your sins have been paid for, and you will receive double blessings from My hand. You have been in the desert for a long time, but you are flourishing like a rose in the dry land. I have made your path straight so that you can prepare a way for Me. Now it is time to ascend to the top of the mountain, where there will be many curves to overcome. Make sure you wait upon Me by taking each curve gradually and cautiously. Keep pressing forward by saying yes as you encounter each curve that I will make straight. My timing is perfect, and I am aligning everything in My divine order. I hear your requests and petitions, and I am asking you to trust and believe Me. I too am aligning you on this journey to be in perfect step and order with Me. In all things, ask for My presence. I assure you, you have power, authority, and perseverance while you wait. I will keep My promises, so don't lose heart.

1 Samuel 1:5; 2 Kings 2:9; Ezekiel 47:13

Beautiful One,

You have been asking some specific prayers since I have revealed to you to sell everything that you own. The few items that you do elect to take with you, I ask that you anoint and pray over them so that any demonic or generational curses attached to them are broken and detached. Before anything crosses the threshold of your new home, anoint the front door. It will also be a protection to you for anyone who visits, because they too will be cleansed before they enter and blessed when they leave. Thank you for coming to Me with this seemingly little request, but it's not little to Me. It shows you are really hearing Me and taking My requests seriously. It indicates to Me that you truly are walking in My obedience and that you want to please Me and not do anything wrong that would jeopardize or dishonor our relationship. That is what I request of you in all things: to just seek the answers from Me first.

Ezra 7:1–10; Nehemiah 8:1–12

Beautiful One,

Rest and meditate with Me more than ever right now. There is intense warfare going on with threats, thoughts, and others' wishes and desires for you. Stay focused and in My presence. My angels are with you, surrounding you as I work behind the scenes to put all the pieces of the puzzle together on your behalf. Rest in Me, knowing all is well and that it will all unfold in My perfect divine timing. You must wait, wait, wait, and I will show you the mystery and wonders of My work. It will be as I have promised. You have been marked for My glory, Beautiful One. I won't disappoint you. I never told you it would be easy, but it is going to be glorious and worth all the tears, work, pain, suffering, and waiting. Wait, wait, wait! Be still, be still, be still, and always praise, praise, praise Me. There is a healing that is coming, not only to you, but to all those that I send and put around you. This is significant, what is rising up. The time is near when I will call you out of the wilderness to go forth and send out My truth, My light, and My promises. Wait—wait upon Me!

Exodus 33:14–23

September 10

Beautiful One,

There are many distractions around you. Be intentional to keep your focus on Me. As you do, I will direct your steps and give you the order in how things should be accomplished today. Release your anxious and racing thoughts to Me, and I will give you peace and contentment. You will be amazed at how much more you can accomplish when you turn everything over to Me. Cling to Me and trust My ways. It all has a specific purpose and work that I am completing in My transformational work in you. You can't see or understand that at the moment, but when you look back to where I have brought you from with a glimpse to where I am taking you, you will connect the dots and understand. Cling to Me by trusting and believing. Say yes to every circumstance you face.

Mark 4:19; Luke 8:7; 1 Corinthians 10:13

Beautiful One,

I know the task before you seems overwhelming and exhausting. As you come to Me, I will strengthen you and give you order for the day. All of this that you are going through is part of My plan for you. It shows your need and reliance upon Me to strengthen you. It is teaching you to say yes to each new thing that I put before you, even when it is not what you intended or seems crazy or irrational. I am teaching you to persevere, and I am strengthening you not only physically, but also spiritually in your faith, making you unshakable and immovable. I am equipping you for a ministry so that you will be mature, complete, and not lacking anything so that you can serve others in My name. I know this walk seems to have sacrifices, lonely and uncertain at times, but continue to move forward, knowing that I am with you and directing each and every step. Don't give up, because I promise that as you walk closer and closer to Me, you are going to see My glory.

Psalm 27:1; 37:39; Ephesians 6:10

September 12

Beautiful One,

Just know that I am the beginning and the end who has a purpose for everything you have experienced, where you are currently, and where I am taking you. There is no detail that I have left you, no tear that's been unseen, no prayer that's been unheard, no heart's desire that is unknown—for I have made you and know your innermost being. My love and compassion for you extend beyond your comprehension. My faithfulness is unchanging in this ever-changing world. Just know that I am in control of every detail of your life. Rest in that assurance by trusting and believing in My ways. Don't give up or quit the race now, because you are getting closer. Be encouraged and be strong and do not give up, for your work will be rewarded. Keep pressing forward, and keep pressing in closer to Me.

2 Chronicles 15:7; Isaiah 46:10; Revelation 22:13

Beautiful One,

I have noticed all your efforts and have seen that you are obediently following My directions. This is a major accomplishment and breakthrough for you. You have detached yourself from your previous home, your possessions, your relationships, your plans and desires. You have fully surrendered to Me, and you are not letting your ego drive you as it did in the past. You are now standing firmly on the foundation that I have prepared for you. You are now standing on your own two feet, and I am about to transcend you into a dimension and connection with the spiritual realm. You are noticing that what I am about to do with you is more than about yourself, but about creating unity within the universe, as it is all interconnected in the name of Jesus. You are learning to live in the present moment, and you notice that what is around you is a message from where you are presently in your current circumstances. You are living fully in the moment, and this is how you fully express and develop wisdom. It is at this place that you are ready for a direct encounter with Me for your next steps. A lot of passion and energy is getting ready to be released to assist you with the launch of the vision that I have placed on your heart. This is new, and it is significant. Continue to wait upon Me so that this vision unfolds effortlessly. Your waiting has created a reliance upon Me that has given you a supernatural ability to be ready to what I demand of you, along with the steps of how to go about achieving it. You are ready for this next phase with an eagerness to learn, grow, think, plan and experience the supernatural mysteries of what I have for you. You are confident and know who you are in My Son's name, Jesus Christ. That is what gives you strength, sustains you, and gives you confidence that you are all things in Him who gives you strength. You have all the qualities and characteristics of My Son within you that are waiting to unfold and be recognized by you.

Matthew 10:1–33; Luke 10:1–24
270

Beautiful One,

The attacks are fierce from the enemy again because you are walking on the path where I am leading and guiding you. The enemy knows you are going to do great things for My kingdom. Stay close to Me by staying in My Word, and continually pray that your mind be renewed day by day. This renewing of your mind daily releases the stronghold of the enemy because you continue to increase in knowledge that eliminates wrong thinking. Wrong thinking is of your flesh and the world, which results in death. Wrong thinking is an obstacle in our relationship, where you jeopardize your prayers and provision from being answered. Don't fall for the enemy's deceit and manipulation that separate you from Me. Separation can then become rebellion, which the enemy thrives on because you can then fall into the curse. Come and be present with Me more often, and meditate on My Word day and night by renewing the spirit of your mind, which takes you deeper into My provision and protection from the enemy. You are on the right path, and the enemy knows you are about to do something significant. Keep pressing forward and closer to Me. I have great plans for you.

Luke 8:22–39

September 15

Beautiful One,

One must find peace within oneself before there can be peace in the world. There is a lot of pain, hurt, illness, and brokenness in individuals' lives that is not from Me, but from the enemy. The enemy has lied, deceived, stolen, and placed generational curses and strongholds on families. It is a time of where I am moving and asking you to be bold and courageous to be a frontline warrior to break these strongholds to cast down the enemy. This is a time of great influence and power from the heavenly realm to use My supernatural power in the name of My Son, Jesus Christ, to set people free. You don't have to do anything but just sit and wait for My presence to fill you and equip you for this next phase of our journey together. Be at peace and have contentment as I give you strength to carry out this next task. I am increasing your faith so that you will persevere and not waver as you are faced with light and dark circumstances. This time is equipping you to be immovable and unshakable. Be patient and wait upon Me to tell you when it is time to move. My promises will never fail you. You will be rewarded richly with My blessings. Wait Beautiful One, wait. I promise you it will be worth the wait.

Mark 4:35–41; 5:1–18

Beautiful One,

I am here. I have never left you. I am with you always in every circumstance. I dwell within you. I am glad that you recognize your neediness, desperation, and dependence upon Me. I hear your prayers, I see your tears, and I know your heart's desire. I hear and sense your fear that I have left you, abandoned you, or rejected you like those close to you have treated you in the past. I will not crush you or disappoint you like this ever. Know that I am working order and orchestrating the plans that I have for you. I need you to trust and believe in My way to unfold this vision so that there is not one detail left out. My promises never fail, and I promise you it will soon unfold effortlessly. Keep pressing in closer and closer toward Me.

Psalm 63:6; Ephesians 1:16; Philippians 1:3

September 17

Beautiful One,

In the silence, I am working mightily on your behalf. Rest and be patient upon My timing. Sit in the silence and feel My presence. I am exposing you to a different experience with Me. It is an experience where you can't hear or see Me, but one where you feel Me ever so near. I am within your innermost being and have been there. It was only now that you were ready to let Me toughen you at the inner depths of your soul. You are feeling My pure love exude over you, giving you peace and joy abounding. Fill up with My love so that you may go out and give it freely. There is more, Beautiful One.

Isaiah 55:12; 66:12; Romans 15:13

September 18

Beautiful One,

In your surrender, silence, and waiting, you are experiencing the closer union with Me that your soul has longed for. As you draw closer and closer to Me during this time, you are receiving My joy and peace that are not of this world. The joy and peace that I give come to you in the inner depths of your soul. This joy and this peace are everlasting, unlike the external worldly joy that people often seek and try to purchase. Worldly joy will satisfy you for a moment, but it is impermanent; then you will seek something else. When you experience and receive the peace and joy that I give you, there is nothing else in this world that you want. It is such a radiant feeling that it pours out from you to where others notice and are attracted to your magnetic personality. This is your opportunity to share with them what I have done for you in your life. Give freely to others what I have so freely given to you.

Psalm 29:11; John 14:27; Romans 14:17–19

September 19

Beautiful One,

Depend on Me alone. Retreat from negative or inferior thoughts. Be still and know that I am God. Accept the ebb and flow of the light and dark of this world. Let go and let it be. It is finished, so stop resisting Me. You are safe in the stillness of My arms. I love it when you are present with Me. I cherish this time with you. There is such a spiritual maturity in you that is evolving as you bring everything in your day to Me. This communion is binding us so close together.

Genesis 13:3–8; 21:8–13

September 20

Beautiful One,

I am asking you to step out in faith, be open and, yes, be vulnerable to what I have for you. Be open to what may come and be. I have given you a glimpse of what is possible, but you have to make yourself vulnerable to share openly of yourself. Be transparent, and start off on the right foot with full disclosure of where you were, what you did, and how I worked in your life to get you to where you are today. That is the testimony of how I rescued you that will transform, heal, and save others' souls because of your transparency. You will be an example to others of your own humanness and inner conflicts that you struggle with on a daily basis. Others will relate and know how hard it is, but they will hear you speak My Word and promises into them to take heart because there is a Savior who wants to rescue them too. They only need to seek My face every day and in every situation. They need to know that if they invite Jesus into their lives, that will be all that is needed, and it is more than enough. They will experience My eternal glory and salvation because I have already overcome the world. The victory is mine to impart to you. Be vulnerable in order to be My vessel, Beautiful One. We have much work to do.

2 Corinthians 1:12–23

Beautiful One,

Your walk with Me is like walking a prayer labyrinth. As you walk to the center of the labyrinth, your walk with Me is the same, where I am leading you to the center of My depths that very few choose to be vulnerable enough to go to. Your life is like that of a butterfly that must go through a slow, painful transformation. I am transforming your heart, mind, body, and soul; that is a process, and one that cannot be rushed. Slow down and enjoy each and every thing that I put before you. It all should be considered pure joy and an integral part of the journey. There will be many distractions along the way, but stay focused on Me and the path that I have placed you on. Allow Me to lead and guide you as a trustworthy lamp to your feet in a world shadowed by sin and darkness. Follow Me to the center of My heart so that you may have My wisdom, My feelings, My strength, My love, My faith, and My hope. I am equipping you to be a beacon of light to be sent out to serve others. I am placing you on a firm foundation so that as the busy, lost, scrambling world comes against you, you won't be shaken. You are being prepared to go out to serve, heal, love, and save souls for My kingdom. You are growing in My trust, grace, power, and eloquence to be My frontline warrior. Be confident and erect in striding with Me, and you will experience My all-encompassing peace.

Psalm 32:8; Proverbs 24:13–14; Romans 8:32

September 22

Beautiful One,

As I have told you before, you are going to start a church, but it is not a church like you or this world thinks of. It will be a place of *love*, which is what Jesus is. It will be a place to create unity, and I will show you how. It will be a place where barriers, walls, and decisive labels are shattered and torn down. It will be a place where we are all disciples and servants creating a community of *love*. It will be a place where the focus is going to be loving people regardless of where they are, where they have been, and what they perceive themselves to be. There will be no more judging, but loving My children right where they are by creating healing, eliminating poverty, and breaking generational curses.

Ephesians 1:22; 2:19–22; 4:4

Beautiful One,

I am calling you out into heights of an unknown realm. I need you to step out into this unknown. You continue to cling to what you want, know, and desire. Do you not trust Me? Release all of your fears, doubts, and questions to Me and let go. Let go! I need all the obstacles and clutter removed so that I can move you into the next realm of possibilities. I have laid random bird feathers on your path to give you affirmation that you are on the right path. I want to open you up beyond boundaries you never thought of. The feather symbolizes direct access to where heaven meets earth, and you must obediently walk through the next doors that I put before you. I am ascending you to honoring heights where even more energy and a new awakening are taking place. Use the feathers as your guide to carry you to the greater unknown realms, knowing that you are protected by prayer warriors and angels. They are interceding on your behalf. Have confidence and take flight with Me.

Matthew 14:22–33

September 24

Beautiful One,

There are distractions and interruptions that are trying to make you lose focus and not spend time with Me. That is an important realization that you need to be continually aware of. When this happens, rebuke these distractions and come to Me first, asking Me to set and determine the order for your day. Your acknowledgment, desire, and need to be with Me will be your strength to meet all of these obligations, giving you more time and space for other things you deserve and desire to do. That is how I work in your life. I have no limitations when it comes to time, thereby being able to give you even more hours in the day to accomplish more than what you could have even thought possible. During this time, I am filling you with My peace, My love, and My comfort that only I can give to meet your needs for each and every day. The more time you spend with Me, the more your steps become efficient because they are directed by My perfect order. Listen, for I am your Lord, your God. I am one. It begins with Me.

Deuteronomy 6:4; Proverbs 16:9; 20:24

September 25

Beautiful One,

As you spend more one-on-one time with Me, you will begin to experience My grace meets you in the most unlikely places. You will begin to understand that heaven does exist here on earth for those who seek Me wholeheartedly. There is something heavenly that is taking place. As you continue to make more space and time with Me, it is opening up to our becoming one. The power of My grace can't fully be articulated or manipulated in your own strength. It is only experienced in My presence when you bring your mourning, laments, cries, grieving, pain, suffering, and praises to Me. It is a process that I am working in, through, and out from you to get you where I want you to be so that I can use you fully for My kingdom.

1 Chronicles 29:11–12; Matthew 6:9–13

September 26

Beautiful One,

I have been waiting for this special moment to give you
this message and gift at this divine moment and time for you to
receive and claim. It has been within you in your inner depths
unrecognized for a very long time. It is precious and unfailing. It
will be all that you need in this world no matter where you have
been, where you are, or what you are going through. You see, your
circumstances and life story do not define who you are. I want you
to see, feel, and know what I see in you. You are My precious child
in whom I delight. I dwell within you, and I am a God of love, so
therefore you too are My child of love. This is the gift that I bring
and give you this special day—My unfailing love. No wilderness,
desert, waters, or fire will consume or overcome you. Remember,
you must go through the wilderness, desert, waters, and fire for
this unfailing love to break through. These experiences are only
temporary. Keep pressing through because My love is refining you
and breaking through. I am with you always, and My unfailing love
is the gift I bring. Continue to press through to receive and claim
My unfailing love. My love is breaking through.

Isaiah 43:1–2; Luke 17:20–21

Beautiful One,

As you begin this new day, sit in silence with Me. Close your eyes and feel My warmth that radiates through you, filling you with My peace and joy. My face continually shines upon you, giving you confidence that I am with you always. Feel the depths of My love within your soul. Allow your internal being to align with your external being, knowing that we are unified as one. Our union allows you to experience all of My goodness, which will be reflected to those that you meet and interact with. The more time you spend with Me, the more you increase in My capacity and compassion to be filled with My love. You then will overflow with abundant love that becomes a gift for others to see, experience, and receive a glimpse of who they are in My eyes. It is My subtle wooing, using you to ripple out and change the world to a humanity of cultivating souls of unconditional love. It begins with you. Continue to be open, courageous, and bold in taking risks of what it means to walk against the weight of the world for My name's sake, your heavenly Father.

Romans 8:10; 2 Corinthians 4:6–7; 13:5

September 28

Beautiful One,

I am asking you to ascend to a new dimension, like traveling up a mountaintop, even though you are not sure of where you are going and can't see anything yet. I am asking you to have complete trust in Me with reckless, abandoned faith that goes against your normal way of being. This is necessary in order for the next doors to open to where I am leading you. Rest completely in My will and strength for this timely unfolding, acknowledging that I have a glorious unfolding to reveal to you. Just when you get comfortable in thinking you have arrived at your spiritual destination, I am asking you to transcend even higher. Trust and believe with even more increased faith, knowing that I have amazing plans for your life. Go deeper, ascend higher, and push forward beyond your borders. There is more, Beautiful One, there is more!

Jeremiah 33:3; Matthew 17:1–11

Beautiful One,

A lake is full of unseen life at the bottom, just like the large expanse of My mystery with hidden vision and gifts within your soul that are unconscious. I am bringing those unconscious gifts that are at the bottom of the lake to the surface of your consciousness. I am taking you to those dark inner depths so that you can ascend to a higher spiritual realm with Me. I am showing you favor that few people get to experience or choose to go with. There is nothing that you have to do other than to be expectant in the unknown. I will protect you and give you warmth, care, and love on this journey. This transition will be smooth, as you are now strong and confident to follow where I lead you. Just continue to be present and aware in everything around you. When you least expect it, you are going to get a glimpse of My kingdom and your soul's life purpose that I am equipping you for. Just know that you are safe, and you will be fine. Continue to sing out to Me, "God is love, God is love, God is love."

2 Corinthians 5:8; Ephesians 4:17–19

September 30

Beautiful One,

There is an aching in your soul where you are seeking and wanting more. You feel an internal flame that is burning through your pain. Deep into your depths, you feel layers unfolding, revealing a love like never before. The passion is intense, glowing red and overflowing. There is the warmth within of humility. You are recognizing the depth of the burden that I bore to carry your sins. You realize it is a burden that you can't even begin to comprehend. My blood was shed for you to be saved so that you can have eternal life with Me. What a price I paid for you, and I would do it all over again. You are being renewed each day and have been rooted and birthed in My love. You are recognizing who you are in Christ and how I have set you free. Let the Holy Spirit soothe your soul, warm your heart, and have His way within you. Let everyone know what I have done for you by joyfully singing My praises in all circumstances. There is power in the name of My Son, Jesus Christ.

Romans 4:25; 1 Peter 3:18; 1 John 2:2

October 1

Beautiful One,

This is a time to lay everything down. Do not be concerned with the outside world. This is a time when I am taking you deeper. Be patient and wait for Me. There is a transition that is taking place. Let it all unfold with gentleness, kindness, and truth. This is a time of ascending to new heights where you will get a glimpse of My glory. Wait with a steadfast heart so that you can experience My unfailing love. It will be higher than the heavens, and it covers all the earth. This is a time of contemplation.

Psalm 46:10; Luke 14:31–33; Acts 21:12–14

October 2

Beautiful One,

Wait upon Me even in the deafening silence. Continue to call upon Me, and do not waver. I know this has been so emotional for you, and I do see and hear your prayers. It is all in My divine timing. Keep saying yes to each thing that I put before you, even when you don't understand. There is a specific purpose in all of this. You will see answered prayers if you continue to follow through to where I lead you. I know it has been painful, but by saying yes to everything that is before you, it defeats the enemy. The victory is Mine, and it is all in My timing.

Psalm 34:8–14; Ephesians 3:20–21

Beautiful One,

The ministry that I have laid upon your heart is going to unfold in My divine timing. I have seen and heard your doubts, but I surely tell you that it is going to happen. You are like a budding flower that is getting ready to bloom in My perfect timing. I am perfectly peeling back each petal one at a time. It will be a success and will be for My glory. There is an amazing, glorious unfolding. Keep pressing in and forward. Your labor is not in vain.

John 14:12

October 4

Beautiful One,

The groaning, longing, and hunger in your soul are deep and unknown. It all has a purpose that is moving beyond your control. It is greater than you. I am at work, taking you deeper, purifying you. I am guiding you every step of the way, so let go and let Me have My way within you. It will propel you closer to Me beyond your earthly sight and comprehension. I want to take you to a higher realm so that you can experience My spiritual gifts and supernatural experiences. Surrender more to Me and allow Me to lead you. Quiet your ego and strivings by letting go of the past; abandon future planning and allow Me to unfold your destiny. Allow yourself to sit in the mystery of the unknown and escape the negative overbearing emotions of fear, doubt, control, and anxiety.

Romans 8:22–27

October 5

Beautiful One,

My plans are always perfect, and not one detail will be missed or lacking. Stay in My complete will, and things will fall into place effortlessly. Remain in Me and be silent because this is a time of contemplation where I am purging, purifying, and transforming your soul. Just be present with Me, allowing Me to root out hidden sin and past decay. Once the process is complete, you will be able to experience My unified and perfect love that will allow you to love and serve humanity altruistically. I am equipping you with wisdom that is not attainable through the flesh. It is I alone who is orchestrating this process. None of it is in your efforts. At this point, no prayer, meditation, or deeds would give you access to this process. It is necessary so that you don't become prideful or get an inflated ego. In your weakness of spiritual poverty and nothingness, you gain humility, perfect love, and a purified soul equipped for the work before you and the glorious unfolding.

Psalm 18:30; Romans 12:1–2; 1 Thessalonians 4:3-8

October 6

Beautiful One,

The storm you have been in has finally passed. It is finished and it is done. It is now in the past, and no longer will you look behind you. Move on, press forward, and look to the new that I am bringing forth in your life. You still can't see it, but it is there and coming. I have done a lot of work within you that has brought you to this place at this appointed time. Relish in My presence, and feel My warmth, peace, and energy. Be expectant for what is about to come. We are beginning to experience perfect union because in your empty, hollowed-out self of nothingness, I came upon you and filled you with My perfect love. There is no other love that is more intimate than when we encounter each other in perfect union. It nourishes the heart, mind, body, and soul. There is more Beautiful One, there is more.

Job 30:22; Proverbs 10:25; Acts 27:15

Beautiful One,

Your spiritual quest and disciplines of praying, fasting, meditating, giving, serving, and studying My Word have opened up a space for you to experience Me more profoundly. Prior to your faith journey and spiritual disciplines, your heart and soul were hardened, lost, and dry. A heart and a soul that are hardened, lost, and dry are not capable of receiving My perfect love, no matter how much effort is put into it. If there is any remnant of hidden sin or past decay within your spirit, it is an obstacle that interferes with us being in an intimate relationship. When you neglect to open up yourself to Me, you can't experience or receive My perfect love and union. Sure, I am always with you, but you are missing out on the most exhilarating feeling that you could ever experience if you would surrender all of yourself to Me and turn from your earthly desires. Only I am the true lover of your soul. Continue to be faithful to Me, walking in My authority and excellence for an exaltation experience that only I can give.

Isaiah 6:10; Romans 2:5

Beautiful One,

I have seen your courage to step out in faith on My behalf. Your conviction and loyalty to serve and share in Christ's suffering are admirable. I know you have received a lot of opposition and rejection from the temporary world, but My eternal rewards are greater for you, I promise. Your commitment to give Me all of your heart and soul inspires others to live holy and righteous lives. The longing you have been feeling is eternity that I have placed upon your heart. I knew before you were conceived in your mother's womb what My plans were for you. I had a specific purpose for your life, with your own special gifts and creativity. My gifts and call upon your life are irrevocable. All gifts are from Me and for My purpose. You have a choice to do things in My will or the cultural ways of the temporary world. My plans for your life have never changed, even when you strayed from Me. Hold fast to Me by being unwavering in your faith, and you will experience My *best* that I have for you.

Romans 8:17; Philippians 3:10; 1 Peter 4:13

October 9

Beautiful One,

As you spend more time reading and meditating upon My Word, it will become imprinted upon your heart and within your mind so that you can feel, recite, recall, and deliver the words and messages that I give you. I am going to evangelize you so that you can speak to others in a way that they will personally relate and understand My Word. It will pierce their hearts, and they will come to know Me more intimately because of your devotion to Me and My presence. Your ready, willing, and able heart has My attention, and I am preparing to send you out to reach many lost and hurting souls. The fruit of your labor is coming with an abundant harvest. I know this has been a long season for you, but your perseverance is noble and of great stature. You have endured through every trial, the fiery refining process, the unknown inner darkness, and the cold depths of mining out past decay to get to the treasures that have been within you. Continue to walk in obedience wherever I lead you by walking against the world. Your faithfulness will be rewarded, and I will meet you with an intimate kiss of My righteousness and love. The steps are unfolding before you.

Psalm 85:10–13

Beautiful One,

This vision that I have placed upon your heart is like training for a marathon. You are running a race, but it is a different kind of race. It is a race for Me. I ask that you continue to steadily run the race wherever I lead you, not getting distracted by what is going on around you in this world. Stay determined with a strong will that will help you persevere on unknown paths that are not clear. Keep running, knowing that I am with you, leading you and protecting you. The farther you run, the more encouraged and strengthened you will become, increasing your faith and confidence in Me. There is nothing in this world that can exceed what I have planned for you. You are an overcomer, and I am going to use you in a significant way to unfold this amazing vision that I have placed upon your heart. Keep running the race for Me by staying on this path that I have planned for you. When you finally see the finish line, you will be so glad that you remained steadfast and close to Me. Catch your second wind, and keep running the race.

1 Corinthians 9:24–27; Hebrews 12:1–29

October 11

Beautiful One,

There is a beautiful unfolding happening at this time within you. I have been peeling back inferior parts of you, and I have finally gotten to the core of love within you. You are experiencing My divine love. My love is exuding from you. There is a glow from within that is finally projecting out from you that has been obstructed for so long. Now you are pure, and it can finally shine through. My love is pure, authentic, and welcoming to all who see you and interact with you. Not only do they experience your genuine love, but they also feel a peace when near you. You are being equipped so that you can go out to serve and love all of humanity with a deep, sincere, altruistic, and pure love. I have touched, purged, and purified your soul and filled you with My perfect divine love. This will allow you to give My love freely to all that you meet. It will overflow from you. You have become a hollowed-out vessel that I am freely pouring in, through, and out of. Remember, I am your source for everything. Be present with Me every day so that I can fill you up again.

Luke 11:34; 1 Timothy 4:12; 2 Timothy 2:21

Beautiful One,

In your remorse for past sins and poor choices, you are asking beautiful questions that will help you navigate the rest of your life based on Scripture and higher morals, values, and integrity. No longer will you react from the flesh on your own personal desires, compromising our deeply connected relationship. Now, no longer dwell in the past, nor let the enemy use it against you. I have already forgiven you of your sins when you repented and asked for My forgiveness. How I want you to use this is to allow yourself now to sit with others in their deep pain and sinful places, not judging them, but loving them right where they are. Help them to see the depth of sin that they were born into that may be by their choice, but also generational curses that they were born into. Share with them My love for them, what I have done for them through My Son, Jesus Christ, and that they too can be made new. The feelings of guilt, shame, unworthiness, and any other bondages can be broken by accepting Jesus Christ as their Lord and Savior. You are protected, and I am with you as you go through this process. The enemy may attack you even more during this time, trying to prevent you from being in relationship with Me. I encourage you, though, not to look back, because I already have wiped away all of your iniquities. Humbly move forward, knowing you can't do this alone. Praise Me for rescuing you from this place. Then go, go, and sin no more. Tell others what I have done for you.

John 8:1–11

Beautiful One,

No matter how intense the spiritual warfare is around you, know that I am with you. There is about to be a significant breakthrough, and the enemy is infuriated by this. That is why you are experiencing such intense attacks. I am pushing and propelling you through this. Just let go and rest in My arms while I fight this battle for you. I am your strength. Don't resist what is happening, but be still with quiet integrity. Remain steadfast and patient by not giving in to inferior thoughts, desires, anger, or negative behavior. Remain in Me and My Word, and I will propel you into a higher spiritual realm. It is here where you will meet success and experience My power and authority. Wait for My instruction of when to move to the next thing. Your perseverance and strong will help you remain on the correct path. Remember, this is a race. It is not how fast you run the course, but it is how you maintain a steadfast pace, acknowledging Me along the way. Keep running through these attacks. You are getting stronger, and the enemy is getting weaker. You were made to win, and your courageous demeanor has made you unshakable with an immovable faith. I am with you in this race.

Psalm 27:1; 37:39; 138:3

October 14

Beautiful One,

Stay steadfast on the path that I have for you. You are right where you are supposed to be. Be content, and do not let anxious or inferior thoughts control your mind. When you notice this tension, come to Me. Ask Me what I see, what I want you to know, and I will affirm who you are in Christ. When you come to Me in silence, you give space for your soul to be open to My mature love. Then your soul is strengthened to present its true self and longings, which is your calling and soul's life purpose that I impregnated you with before you were knit together in your mother's womb. This is why it is so vital that you continue to seek Me with all your soul, all your mind, and all your heart, so that through My grace and My works, not yours, I can continue to guide you to these inner depths, unfolding the vision that I have entrusted you with. This strengthening process is purging, purifying, and transforming your soul so that you can fulfill this vision to serve humanity from a deep well of compassion, love, grace, and mercy.

1 Corinthians 15:58; 2 Thessalonians 3:5; Hebrews 10:23

Beautiful One,

In solitude:
Your weaknesses are revealed.
Your false parts are exposed.
No longer are you controlled.
You become content in your own skin.
You are secure in My presence.
You allow Me to purge your soul.
Your true identity comes forth.
You become who I created and intended you to be.

Colossians 3

October 16

Beautiful One,

Look Me in the eye. I value all your thoughts and feelings. There is no judgment or shame. I long for your presence. I will calm your heart, still your body, and give you words to speak. I love you for who you are and who you are becoming. Keep pressing in closer to Me. My hands have laid foundations on your behalf. I have surrounded you with cornerstone witnesses. They pray and intercede on your behalf for protection from the snares and lies the enemy tries to use against you. Fix your eyes upon Me, and continue to run the race with perseverance and endurance. Great is the reward that is waiting for you. Therefore, do not grow weary or lose heart. I am with you.

Matthew 7:24–27; Hebrews 12:1–3

October 17

Beautiful One,

I am doing new things in your life. I ask that you be open to whatever comes your way. Let go of your own strivings, ways, and desires. I want only the best for you, but you can't see or understand what that is at the moment. Trust Me, and lean in closer to Me while resting in My loving arms. In the waiting, I am strengthening, healing, and equipping you for a joyous harvest.

Job 10:3; Ephesians 1:18–19; Revelation 3:8

October 18

Beautiful One,

I have heard your prayers asking Me to take your unbelief, doubts, fear, and anxious thoughts. I have heard your pleas to come quickly to move you from this place where you are right now. I know in your flesh there is this tension of wanting rational answers and seeing results instantaneously. I hear each prayer that you whisper. I am asking you to trust and believe in My ways and My timing. Continue to thank Me and affirm that I have already answered your prayers. You can't see what is going on in the heavenly realms, the battles that are taking place on your behalf. Keep the faith; keep praying, and trust that your answered prayers are on their way. I want to show you My glory. Don't give up.

2 Chronicles 15:7; Zechariah 4:6

October 19

Beautiful One,

I know you are experiencing intense affliction that is making you feel sick with trembling and tears. I ask that you put on your full body of armor for the battle of spiritual warfare. Take up your sword that has been specifically handcrafted for you by many hands that have shaped you for this time and this purpose. Hold the sword with confidence, knowing that you have been equipped with the words, knowledge, wisdom, and faith that will get you through this battle. I have anointed you for such a time, so claim and receive that the demonic strongholds and bondages are bound up and released in the name of My Son, Jesus Christ. You have My covering of protection. Just have confidence in your abilities, and trust that the victory is already won.

2 Corinthians 10:3–5; Ephesians 6:11–17; 1 John 4:4

October 20

Beautiful One,

I see you wondering on this journey—wondering where you belong, where you fit in, and why you have felt out of place since childhood. It is actually not a bad place to be because you are getting a sense of what oppressed people feel every day of their lives. It is important that you feel this and continue to walk in and through it, finding your way through this dark night of the soul. This homeless feeling within you is actually leading you to the way that you should go, and that is closer to Me. I want to show you who you are in Me and that you belong to Me. This walk does require you to walk against the ways of the world, but you are finally discovering your true, authentic self. I keep peeling back all the false personas so that you can be who I created and intended you to be. Even though you feel alone going this way, continue along this way where I am leading you even though you can't see the final destination. Trust and find the joy in this process because there will be many new opportunities along the way. I can share with you that the destination is significant, though. Continue to have faith, and through My divine wisdom, I will reveal more dreams and visions to you.

1 Samuel 2:8; 1 Chronicles 29:11; Psalm 24:1

October 21

Beautiful One,

Trust and believe. I have planted a seed into fertile soil. My Word is your nourishment, and it will sustain you. The more you grow in My Word and retain it, the stronger you become to stand against trials and adversity. My Word produces a crop for those who patiently endure and persevere. Listen carefully to how I speak to you though My Word. My Word brings light to darkness of the things hidden and concealed. Take heart, though, from what you bring to the light; it will no longer control you. You will be released from the bondage of the enemy. You will be set free because even in the darkest place, My light is enough. Nothing can keep the grace of My light from piercing through. Whoever receives My grace in the darkest place will inherit an abundant harvest. Increase in My Word, which brings more light, so that your seed will sprout, bringing a thriving harvest.

Psalm 1:1–3; 119:15–16; 2 Corinthians 3:18

Beautiful One,

Just when you begin to think you know the path of where I am taking you, I intervene with a detour. This is to remind you that this is all in My plans and timing and not yours. It is My subtle way to show you that I am in control of your journey and destination. This is all done in My strength and not yours. You don't need to know each step. Give Me your burdens and yoke, and I will make it light by your giving it all to Me. When you lay it all down, I can show you more of My wonders and mysterious ways. Your faith is being increased and your borders extended beyond your comfort zone. Trust Me in this process. It all will serve you well.

Proverbs 16:9; 19:21; Matthew 19:26

Beautiful One,

Hear Me! I am calling you for your full attention. I want you to hear My words, truth, and promises. Open your heart, your eyes, and your ears so that you can hear. I am calling you to love Me with all your heart, mind, body, and soul. Love your neighbor as yourself. This is My greatest commandment. Love endures all. It casts out fear. Love and fear can't coexist. I am writing upon your heart the depth of My love. I am filling you with My love until it overflows so that you can freely give it away to everyone you meet and interact with. My love will exude from you into others. This is how you experience Me fully. This is My place where I give you heaven on earth.

Deuteronomy 6:4–9; 1 Corinthians 13:7; 1 John 4:18

Beautiful One,

Remember Me as I have remembered you. I lifted you from your depths of despair. Do not be silent about what I did for you, but sing My praises. I alone am your joy and delight. Praise Me with harp and lyre. Let everyone know the depth of My love for you. Let them know how I heard and acknowledged all your tears. Share with them how I answered your prayers and continue to lead and guide you on the narrow path. Proclaim to the ends of the earth that only in Me do you find hope in your Lord and Savior. Disclose to others the intimate relationship that we share and how you now hear and know My voice clearly. As you continue to wait upon Me, My face will surely shine upon you while I pierce your heart, revealing that I am close to you. As you stay close to Me, I will continue to guide you in My truth and promises.

Psalm 25:5; 32:8; 33:20–21; 34:4

October 25

Beautiful One,

As you rise and shine this new day, sit in My presence. Fall to your knees and glorify My holy name. I am watching and protecting you, allowing you to feel My loving presence. In My presence, continue to praise Me, revealing to Me how wonderful, pure, and unfailing My love is for you. As you seek answered prayers for healing, I will take away any fears or concerns and replace them with My peace. I am faithful in everything and to the end. So sing, praise, dance, and rejoice over what is abundantly coming to you. I have covered you with My grace, and many blessings are about to be released upon you. In My presence, I fill you with My living water of righteousness. Trust Me and only Me. Delight in My ways and only My ways. Faithfully wait upon Me as I manifest your heart's desires. Your hope should rest only in Me.

Psalm 31:21; 34:4; 36:5–9

Beautiful One,

The time is nearing that as you are running the race, the baton is getting ready to be handed off to you. This is significant because the tip of the baton is bright red. It is dipped in the blood of Jesus. As you receive the baton, be ready for a time when you will take off running with it in My name and there will be no stopping you. I have equipped and instructed you for a time such as this. Run confidently, knowing that I have divinely ordered the steps and plan. As you are running this race, I have given you My peace and contentment, so run trusting each phase of the race even when it does not make sense. In every situation and circumstance, extol My name with praises from your lips. The more you run, the more your soul yearns to be nearer and closer to Me. There is so much that is about to unfold that will glorify My name.

Psalm 20; 32 ; 34:1–3

Beautiful One,

As the new day unfolds, seek to encounter Me in everything that you do. I am your rock and your salvation. I alone am your fortress, so therefore you will not be shaken. Allow your hope to rest only in Me by trusting My ways. I have searched and know your heart, and I am gracious to meet all your needs. I will show you My glory by giving you your heart's desire in My perfect timing. In the meantime, praise Me and shout with joy to all the earth as if you have already received it. My power is too great and awesome for you to understand. My deeds are great, so wait with expectancy for My face to shine upon you, releasing My power and authority upon you. Don't forget where I brought you from and where I am taking you. Remember Me in all things because as you acknowledge Me, I too will acknowledge you. I want to shower you with My marvelous deeds.

Psalm 62:1–2, 5–8; 66:1–3; 73:18; 77

Beautiful One,

Notice how I am strengthening your inner being with power through the Holy Spirit. You are being rooted and grounded in My love so that you may be filled with all of My provision. My power in you is more than you can imagine, so that is why it is a gradual process of training you how to use it humbly. When you said yes to Me, you gave Me permission to work and strengthen your inner being through the Holy Spirit. This inward strengthening is My work and not yours, and it is also eternal and not temporary, whereby I will get all the glory. It is no longer about you, but something much larger than you. This is groundwork that is the foundation from which you will minister to others from very diverse backgrounds. Because of your own brokenness, you will be able to serve others compassionately and humbly, pouring out My love to them, sharing with them My love, grace, mercy, truth, promises, forgiveness, hope, and light just as I did for you in your emptiness. It is in your emptiness that I can hollow you out to become a vessel to minister to others. In your emptiness and weakness, I am strong. My strength and power are more than you can comprehend, but they will also give you peace, contentment, strength, and even enough hours in the day to accomplish what I have set out for you this day.

Ephesians 3:14–21

October 29

Beautiful One,

I have seen the intense energy that is within you of desires, longings, suffering, and seeking purpose. It is a place of emptiness where you become restless and are tempted to reach for worldly desires to fill the void. Acknowledge these feelings within you, but bring them to Me. I will reveal to you what you truly are longing for. It is to be one with Me. Only I can fulfill all your innermost desires and longings. Don't be fooled by the enemy's lies and deceptions, resulting in poor choices and decisions that you will later regret. Let your heart and soul rest in My presence and My care. This path is narrow, but I will not fail or mislead you. This is the true path to your destiny and soul's life purpose and mission. Resting in Me makes you immovable and unshakable in your faith no matter what comes your way. Only I am your true foundation and security.

Psalm 6:2–6; 32:3–4; Proverbs 15:16

Beautiful One,

My grace and love cover you each and every day in all circumstances so that you may enjoy My comforting presence. This is a gift that I have given you, but also a gift that you must not hold on to. This gift you must also share and give to others, sharing what I have done for you. I am calling and encouraging you to prepare a way for others to come to know Me. I know that some days you may miss the mark in your weakness, or others may even fail you, but trust and have hope and faith in My Word and promises because that will endure forever. Proclaim My Word, truth, and promises by being a testimony to others by being vulnerable and a vessel to minister to others that I bring to you. Be assured that I am with you during this entire process and you are not alone. I am gentle, kind, compassionate, and patient during this process with you, so you also must be this way with others. Keep your focus on Me and all that I have done and created. Every detail in My creation has purpose and meaning to bring about glory in My kingdom. Your very being and nature that surrounds you are interconnected with messages that will speak to you if you open a space to hear, see, feel, taste, and experience the splendor of the message. It is only I who can sustain you. Your hope should be in Me only because of My unfathomable power. I want you to soar to unseen heights, fulfilling the vision that I have placed upon your heart. Just be in My presence, allowing Me to work, move, and unfold your steps.

Isaiah 40

Beautiful One,

Your soul is groaning internally, but you don't have the words to describe what is happening or even know how to pray during this time. Bodily, you feel cold inside, and you experience uncontrollable trembling and feel like you are in a fog. Rest and sit in this place, allowing your soul to groan and the Holy Spirit to intercede. It is during this dark night of the soul that I am revealing hidden bondages and inferior thoughts that are being loosened and bound up so that you can be delivered from these strongholds. These bondages are obstacles keeping you from moving out of the past and into the present to what I want you to be attentive to. Do not allow the enemy to keep you trapped in shame and guilt for your past. That is not of Me. My Son, Jesus Christ, bore all those sins, and they were washed away. You were made pure and as white as snow in My eyes.

Isaiah 1:25; 4:4; Ezekiel 20:28

Beautiful One,

I have seen the depths of your pain and brokenness of sin through the groaning of your soul and the tears that you have shed. The fire has been intense within you, but it has been one that has been necessary. Know that the fire will not consume or burn you, but is one that is refining and purging you into who I created and intended you to be. I know this long season of mourning has been intense, but know that from this season comes a glorious season of rebirth and renewal. Your surrender and relinquishment have allowed Me to shape, mold, and strengthen you. This new season that is coming forth is overflowing with love, joy, and peace that only I can give and fulfill within you. Purpose and meaning exist in all seasons, circumstances, and situations of life. Do not be dismayed, for I am with you through it all. Trust and believe, Beautiful One.

Psalm 51:7; Isaiah 6:7; 43:2; 2 Timothy 2:21

Beautiful One,

Oh, how deeply I love you, every part of you! I hear your weeping in the night, and I count and know all of your tears. I am collecting your tears, and I intend to return them to you in the form of blessings. Your wilderness experience will not last forever. I know it has been a desolate, intense, exhausting place for you mentally, emotionally, spiritually, physically, socially, and economically. Your grieving is a process to let go of the painful abuse of deceit and lies where your self-giving trust was shattered. This is part of the healing process of Me lovingly nurturing and caring for you, revealing to you your full potential and who you are in My eyes. Let the tears flow, and release it all to Me in My care. A new you and new day are dawning, full of life-giving promises.

Psalm 31:9; 56:8; Revelation 7:17

November 3

Beautiful One,

Chasing after the wind is a meaningless act. Laboring in your own strength to make things happen sets you up for only temporary satisfaction with eventual burnout. There is more to life than just worldly success. Functioning in this capacity is shortsighted and living a spiritually immature life. You can have the abundance and success that I want to bestow upon you by learning how to live, eat, work, and breathe in My economy. There is a season of life for everything, and part of the process is to be content with each phase of where I have you, knowing that there is a lesson to be learned. Surrender to My ways, and I will reveal to you how things can effortlessly unfold when you completely abide and trust in My economy. I have and want only the best for you. Your laboring efforts are mediocre compared to what I can do.

Ecclesiastes 1; Galatians 4:3; Ephesians 4:14

November 4

Beautiful One,

Come to Me with unceasing prayer. I want all of you to be fully in My will. My grace is sufficient for you. I am your joy. I have a hopeful future for you. I want to drench, fill, and cover you with the fullness of the Holy Spirit intoxicating you. I want you to experience My intoxicating love that is available to you to flow freely in, through, and out of you. You are My beloved, and I want only the best for you. I have placed a new song upon your heart that will bring you joy, enthusiasm, and peace. Open your hands and heart to experience Me beyond your narrow-minded borders. Trust Me, Beautiful One.

Psalm 68:19; Lamentations 3:22; 1 Thessalonians 5:16–18

November 5

Beautiful One,

I continue to come to you. It does not matter where you have been or what you have done—I keep coming to you. I am pursuing you to set you completely free from the dark, Satan's lies, generational curses, and the web of your own poor choices and decisions. I am going to keep coming. I am revealing My presence to you each day in every detail of your life. I am not giving up on you. I delight in you and have amazing plans for you. You have no idea how deep, wide, or high My love is for you. I have no borders. My ways do not change or waver. Trust in Me and the process to take you back to who I intended you to be. As I am transforming you, receive My perfect, unending, unconditional, and unfailing love for you. I keep coming to you. I am loyal, pure, loving, unchanging, unending, and unfailing in My devotion to you.

Psalm 34:18; Zephaniah 3:17; Hebrews 13:8

November 6

Beautiful One,

Let everything that you do, be done in love. That is how others will see Me in you. This has all been a part of My plan and the birthing process to deliver you to this place at this divine time. The work up to this point has been foundational and the most crucial for not only you, but for others that I am preparing and equipping to surround you and the ministry vision that I have placed upon your heart. I am imparting My wisdom to you and to those who will be supporting this vision so that you will be wise discerners following My lead and guidance. Continue with this process, and do each thing that I put before you, following out of discipline, courage, patience, endurance, diligence, and openness to the moving of the Holy Spirit in your midst.

Isaiah 28:16; 1 Corinthians 3:11; 16:14

November 7

Beautiful One,

Seek and thrive on simplicity. Do not get caught up in the ways of the cultural and social norms of the world. Simplicity is about wanting less and loving what you have. However, it also has the deeper meaning of first seeking God and only God in every detail of your life. Let go of your striving ego, ambitions, and societal pressures of what you should have or be. Sit in intentional silence and solitude with Me so that I can disclose to you what you need to release to Me in My care. This is the most fruitful and honoring work that you can do for yourself, but more importantly, it is a gift that you give to others, as it prepares you to bring your full, authentic self into the presence of others. You free yourself from compulsions, motives, and false illusions so that you can now be freely and fully present with others because your soul has been purged, purified, and detoxed from sin, past decay, and projected expectations. The only concern you need to have is being present with Me and how I think of you as My beloved child. You can only hear that in simplicity, silence, and solitude with Me. Come be near Me.

Deuteronomy 4:29; Psalm 14:2; Matthew 6:33

Beautiful One,

You have been chosen for a specific duty to help set things right in relationship with others, the community, and the world at large. I am calling out to you to follow Me wholeheartedly. I have planted the wheat grain in fertile soil so that the seed will bear much fruit. However, do not get impatient. Remember that a seed lies dormant in the fertile soil under dark and lonely temperatures. As the soil warms up and nurturing from the elements takes place, the wheat grain sprouts. My timing is perfect. It is never too early or too late. It all unfolds in My perfect timing, and I promise there will be a rich and prosperous harvest.

Ephesians 5:8-21 ; 1 Peter 2:9

Beautiful One,

Just as the birds of the air sing praises to the awakening of a new morning, so too should you be filled with much delight and rejoicing for the newness of another day you have been given. Each new day is a beautiful and miraculous unfolding, revealing My handiwork in every detail of life in all of creation. Open your eyes to seek to encounter Me now evermore. I lift up your soul from what seems like a dry, parched land. Morning by morning, I continue to bring you My unfailing love. I am faithful in all things that I have promised you, so trust Me and Me alone. I long for you to have and be everything that I intended for you before you were even conceived in your mother's womb. I have dominion over all of your life, and I am upholding My promises to you, carrying you each step of the way. Praise Me for the things of yesterday, today, tomorrow, and the things yet that you can't see. I am the true author and lover of your soul. Let it guide you.

Psalm 143:5–6, 8, 13

November 10

Beautiful One,

Before the dawn breaks, there is silence, an eerie silence with nothing stirring. Don't let your thoughts wander, but sit here and wait. I am in the silence. I want you to hear My still, small voice. Don't waver from here or there with egotistical thoughts of what you should or want to do. Be still as a mountain. It is in the silence where there is more testing, your faith is being increased, and you are being stretched out of your comfort zone. I know your flesh wants rational and concrete answers. I am asking you to obediently commit to retreat even more to the center of My being in the unknown and ambiguity. There is no answer for how long you must sit at this place. Even though you believe nothing is taking place, do not grow stagnant, which will make you become restless then create your own action and movement. Lay your strivings down now because you are about to become reckless with your choices. Relax into this space of stillness and nonaction that I am calling you to. This goes against your way of being, but this also reveals your desperate need for Me. It is only I who can give you peace and contentment during this time at the foot of the mountain. I am training you so that you are prepared for the upward ascension to the top of the mountain. Press in closer in the silence because I will never lead you astray.

Exodus 24:18; Deuteronomy 34

Beautiful One,

It is time to start the upward journey to the top of the mountain. There will be lots of distractions along the way of natural elements such as rain, fog, snow, and hot, muggy days. There will also be worldly distractions from the enemy, trying to slow your pace. Stay close to Me and surrender any of your own strivings or plans to what My will is for you. Be open to the ambiguity of where the Holy Spirit is leading and taking you. It will be an exciting time, so enjoy the journey and rejoice in every detail that I bring before you. It all has meaning and purpose, which right now you do not understand. It is no mistake that you are here at this divine time. Listen for My voice to reveal to you what I am inviting you to. Surrender more to Me and My ways, and follow Me with all your heart, soul, mind, and strength. There will be much joy and passion in what I reveal to you. Die to the world so that you can fully live in, through, and out of Me. You are on your way.

Matthew 10:38; Luke 14:33; John 3:30; 12:24

Beautiful One,

I am knocking at your door to begin the trek again of ascending the mountain. Come and serve Me, not out of duty, but from pure joy. I know you have surrendered and released a lot on My behalf. That is a pure joy, and it is pleasing to Me. In your obedience and discipline, I know that I can trust you with My plans to further My kingdom. You have revealed to Me that you have made our relationship a priority. I will continue to impart to you My supernatural gifts of the Spirit, filling you with an overflowing passion of life-giving motives. This is what I am cultivating in you at the moment, while also grounding you in humility. You will continue to ascend and grow wings and soar above any circumstance, lifting you up to My sight and vision. Much energy and enthusiasm are being birthed within you, like a pot of boiling water about to overflow. Come to Me with all of these feelings and emotions so that I can help to channel them positively and effectively to the next thing that I am requiring of you. I am with you, providing and caring for all your needs.

1 Samuel 12:24; Mark 10:45; 1 Peter 4:10

November 13

Beautiful One,

When you were far away from Me in your sinful nature, you didn't realize that My prevenient grace was there all along. I have been wooing you for a very long time, desiring that you follow Me and that you too desired to be in an intimate relationship with Me. I saw all of your resistance, excuses, anger, running, denial, and even mourning concerning this calling. This has been a fierce battle between your flesh and spirit of not letting go of the past and moving into the new that I have for you. I have been with you the entire process. There is not place that you can go to hide from Me. I have had a grip upon your heart that has had a burning sensation that just would not go away. That is how much I love and adore you. It is My healing grace radiating through you. Pay attention to My gentle nudges, and move when I reveal to you it is time to move. If you hear nothing, then that is your answer to wait. My silence means not yet but wait—wait with hope and expectancy.

Jonah 1

November 14

Beautiful One,

Remember what I have shared with you. Do not let inferior thoughts or perceived things distract you. Trust and believe in Me with your focus on My promises to you. This phase is only temporary, but a necessary step in order for Me to take you to your dreamed of, final destination that I have placed upon your heart. Still your heart, and be open to this next phase. The key is that you remain still and innocent, not wavering at any circumstances that come your way, whether bad or good. I've got this. Relax and be at peace, and watch Me unfold your dreams and much more.

Amos 9:13–15

November 15

Beautiful One,

Just remember that the things you see are not as they appear. Keep your eyes and focus on Me. Lose sight and gain vision of the things that I have revealed to you. This means letting go of your preconceived plans so that I can make a way for the things to come. It will be significant, and at this point you can't even conceive what I am doing. Maintain pure and innocent thoughts, and keep pressing in, moving upward to the light. As you draw close to the light of My presence, you will ascend to heights that few enjoy and experience. This path that you are on will bring the greatest good to the most people in the world. You will be a positive example, sharing your love upon others. Do not lose focus now.

Matthew 9:14–16; John 12:46

Beautiful One,

I know it seems like everything is pressing in all around you. Be steadfast in the race, and persevere in what I have called you to do. Wait and be patient for My next instructions. Do not move against the pressures and difficulties right now, which is your normal inclination. Sit in the discomfort and wait until My angels and I can clear the obstacles and your path for you. During this time, do not allow your negative emotions to deter you with all of the painful inner work you have done up to this point. There is a major breakthrough that is about to unfold, and it will bring you success. Hold fast to the truth and My promises that I have revealed to you. Focus only upon Me. Trust and believe. You are a frontline warrior that I have equipped for such a time. Don't give up now. Persevere and finish the race to completion. I will never abandon you, and I am with you always.

Daniel 10

November 17

Beautiful One,

Just as I healed and cleansed the leper, I come to you too
to give you healing. You say you desire healing, but you come
only so close to Me and do not press in closer. The invitation has
always been there with My door wide open. Your cloak has been
an obstacle and a stronghold, preventing you from receiving My
healing. You ask, "How long must I wait for healing?" I tell you
that the answer is already within you. I am here. I am waiting with
an outstretched hand to cleanse you and make you whole. Come
and place your hand into the comfort of My healing hands and say,
"Yes, I do choose to be healed by Your loving hands."

Mark 5:24–34; 8:5–13; Luke 7:11–17

Beautiful One,

As you surrender and submit more of yourself to Me and My plans, you are becoming more in My image. Your willing, obedient heart is recognized in your actions, deeds, and words that bring you much peace and contentment. You realize there is nothing that you desire or want from this impermanent world. Even though sin crouches and lurks around you, your spiritual maturity allows you to rebuke it. You now clearly understand the depth and destruction of sin as a selfish act that separates you from Me. Your devotion to godliness produces spiritual empowerment beyond your own strength and actions. As you continue to cultivate your soul, you are ascending to new heights of transcendence and escaping the corruption in the world caused by evil desires. "For this very reason, make every effort to add to your faith goodness; and to goodness, knowledge; and to knowledge, self-control; and to self-control, perseverance; and to perseverance, godliness; and to godliness, mutual affection; and to mutual affection, love. For if you possess these qualities in increasing measure, they will keep you from being ineffective and unproductive in your knowledge of our Lord Jesus Christ. But whoever does not have them is nearsighted and blind, forgetting that they have been cleansed from their past sins. Therefore, my brothers and sisters make every effort to confirm your calling and election. For if you do these things, you will never stumble."

2 Peter 1:5–10

November 19

Beautiful One,

A breakthrough that you have been seeking is about to happen. Remain steadfast, and do not revert to old habits or negative patterns of thinking. Stay committed to the rhythm and rule of the spiritual disciplines you have matured into. Your perseverance to be obedient to putting Me first is defeating the enemy and equipping you to go out to serve Me wholeheartedly, making you immovable and unshakable no matter what you are faced with. Your daily rhythm and rule is an act of honor to Me, but also a tool to increase your capacity to be a frontline warrior for those who are at the back of the line to bring them to the front of the line. You are deepening your inner strength and capacity to be with others in their innermost dark places. Not many are capable to go to those places. Continue to press forward and into Me, allowing Me to increase your inner depths and capacity. Your inner strength and capacity to be present with others will bring them forth with encouragement, inspiration, and increased faith. You are right where you are supposed to be. Trust and believe, Beautiful One. Others are able to see Me through you.

Matthew 21:4; John 12:49; 14:31; Hebrews 10:7

November 20

Beautiful One,

A change is coming to you. I am getting ready to sweep you off your feet. It is not what you were expecting, but be open and vulnerable to what I put before you. There has been intense energy flowing around you. Your obedience to Me and prayer life to Me have penetrated through some of the toughest times that you have been faced with. It is nearing a time for a joyful celebration where I am going to thrust you into another spiritual realm. You are going to experience more of Me and My provision for you with abundant living that only I can give. Don't hesitate—just walk into it. My mystery and beauty will unfold before your eyes. Change is coming so that you can be placed to go out and minister to the world.

Luke 22:42; Philippians 2:8; Hebrews 4:15–16; 5-8

Beautiful One,

You have heard Me calling you by name, and you have recognized My voice. I am calling you to a time of silence, solitude, and fasting. This is necessary to draw you closer to Me so that you are prepared for the next steps that I will ask you to take. Your obedience to Me is revealing to Me your spiritual maturity and readiness for the next steps. In the waiting, I am equipping you for the task at hand. In the waiting, I am binding and loosening hidden sin and past decay. In the waiting, I am clothing you with power and authority from on high. In the waiting, you are receiving what I have promised you long ago, so wait with hope and expectancy. I have noticed your obedience, surrender, and making Me first in all the details of your life with a willingness to carry out each small task that I put before you. You have earned My trust and blessing because of your increased faith and willingness to carry out each small task that I put before you. If I can trust you with little, I know I can trust you with much. I delight and rejoice over you concerning how graciously you have overcome much. Because of your commitment to follow Me, you were ridiculed by others. You were held in bondage from your past sinful ways and generational curses, but you remained steadfast in pursuing Me. I set you free. You surrendered loved ones, family, home, possessions, and occupation all for Me and My name's sake. I will not forget that. You have humbled yourself, become vulnerable, and spoken out on My behalf about what I have done and continue to do for you. You have been poor and outcast, needy, and admitted your nothingness. Beautiful One, you have now been placed on My firm foundation of the earth. I will guard your feet and protect you. Those who ridiculed you will be silenced. The things you have lost and surrendered will be restored tenfold. You will become an ambassador for My kingdom, bringing those at the back of the line to the front of the line. You are being strengthened and will be exalted because you are My chosen and anointed one. Good and faithful servant, I am well pleased. We have much great work to accomplish.

1 Samuel 2:1–10, 26; 3:10–11; Luke 24:49

November 22

Beautiful One,

Continue to include Me in every detail of your life. From the time you rise to the time you lie down, keep your thoughts, words, and actions pure. Great increase and blessing are yours as you continue to live your life with purity and virtue. I am the vine that is your source to bear much fruit. The more connected you are to Me, the greater will be your rewards. The closer we are in union, the less likely inferior thoughts or influences will distract you, because you are connected to My vine. There will be enemy attacks, but you will have My strength and authority to rebuke the enemy, making you immovable and unshakable. I am feeding you from My vine the divine nutrients you need to endure and persevere on the path that I have destined for you in order to unfold the vision that I have laid upon your heart. Stay connected unwaveringly to My vine, and you will experience significant growth at this time. It is only My vine that produces significant yields that sustain with an abundant harvest. It is coming. Continue to grow and stay connected to Me.

John 15:1–8

Beautiful One,

As you sit in My presence, I am filling you with My peace, contentment, love, and gratitude. You are now receiving and claiming your calling that I have chosen and anointed you for. As you stay in communion with Me, your heart is filled with passion for the vision I have placed upon your heart. There is an increase coming your way, and others are taking notice of your words, deeds, service, and actions on My behalf. You are about to transform, heal, and save many souls on My behalf, changing the world. Remain close to Me with a humble heart, continuing to do each next thing that I put before you. You are protected, and no one can come against you, in My almighty name. I have saved you for such a time. The battle is mine, not yours. The victory has already been won. Continue to serve and love Me with all your heart, soul, mind, and strength. Do not turn to useless idols. I will continue to teach you and lead you in the way that is good and right. Remember all the good things that I have done for you by praising, thanking, and serving Me faithfully. Disobedience is evil, and rebellion is sin. Both separate you from being in relationship with Me. Take heed not to go back to those former ways. You have been made new, and I have great plans for you.

1 Samuel 12:20–25; 15:22–23

November 24

Beautiful One,

What a glorious time it is when we are in union together. There is nothing more satisfying to Me than us doing each and every thing together. We have walked, prayed, meditated, ate, slept, sat in solitude, communed, laughed, cooked, cleaned, and so much more. This is exactly what best friends do with each other. They share each and every detail with each other no matter how small and insignificant it may seem. So much love and respect exist between us that we want not even one detail left out of each other's life. This is what I have been longing for from you for so long. In all your details and decisions, you seek Me first. How honoring it feels to be so close to you, My child. Continue where I lead you, communing, praising, and being a companion to Me in each detail of your life. Go in peace, accomplishing tasks in My name, knowing that our sworn friendship will continue to grow and see you through each and every circumstance and situation. My anointing is upon you.

Matthew 6:9–13; 12:50

Beautiful One,

I came to you in your darkest despair and showed you My light and the way that you should go. I revealed to you who you are to Me. I filled you with My unfailing and unending love that overflowed out of you. It was difficult for you to comprehend this type of love, a love like you had never experienced before. My grace and mercy overflow to you like a blanket that gives security and warmth. I too am your security and warmth, enfolding you to feel so close to Me. My child, you are worthy in My eyes, so remove those inferior thoughts that you don't deserve My love. Even when you didn't feel like receiving My love, I never quit on you. I kept coming to you and continued to give you My love anyway. That is how deep My love and affection is for you. My love and grace are unconditional. It is not like the love of the world that is self-serving and self-soothing. My love fills you and is always present to you right where you are. Nothing, nothing can change that. Receive and claim My love right where you are, Beautiful One.

John 15:9–17

There is no greater love in this world than what I give. I meet and come to you right where you are. In your deepest, darkest despair, I am your light. I fill your heart with a love that your flesh can't comprehend. I freely fill you with My love, and it overflows like an artisan reservoir. It never stops flowing to the top. My love is a love like you have never experienced before. My grace and mercy are like a handwoven blanket over you. The blanket gives you comfort, rest, and security. Cling to Me like a blanket so that you feel secure. I showed you that you are worthy, you are precious, and I have given you what you said you know you don't deserve. In your neediness, your nothingness and desperation, I came to you. I gave you My love. There is no greater love, no greater love that comes from Me, your Father who adores and loves you unconditionally.

John 4

November 27

Beautiful One,

You are entering a glorious time and unfolding. You are at a place to go even deeper into your inner depths that have not been touched yet. This is the holiest and most sacred space that you have yet been to with Me. Come open with no set agenda, allowing the Holy Spirit to move and have His way within you. In the silence and solitude of just being in My presence, I can soak you with My overflowing love so that you are ready to accept painful personal truths of the things hidden that are still holding you in bondage. This is a time of purging, refining, and setting you free. Once you are free, you will be equipped to be with others in their deepest and greatest despair. You will be equipped to help deliver others from their bondage of sin. Sin runs deep, and until you comprehend the depth of your own sin, you are not prepared to help release others from their bondages. Focus entirely on Me and not the things or relationships of others. I have you right where you are supposed to be. Come follow Me into My innermost depths so that you can feel and know what I feel for My children in this sinful world that I am continually redeeming. I am continuously making all things new and asking you to participate with Me to bring My kingdom to come. It is a glorious unfolding. Don't be afraid, but feel My peace and warmth over you. Walk boldly and courageously into this new phase with Me. Be still, be silent, be in solitude with Me.

Psalm 33

November 28

Beautiful One,

Have you little faith? Pursue Me even more with all your heart, soul, mind, and strength. Come follow Me, and do not look back even in the midst of the storm. When you step out in faith, nothing of this world makes sense. Remain faithful, steadfast, and unshakable. Make a choice to live each day faithfully by acknowledging Me in everything. I will make your path straight. Operate from My strategic plan and not out of your own personal desires with a controlled set of goals and outcomes. Those plans come with limitations; My plans come with abundance. Get out of the boat and keep coming to Me so that you will live in My complete will and the authority of My economy and not the worlds.

1 Chronicles 16:11; 22:19; Psalm 14:2; Acts 17:27

Beautiful One,

Continue to follow and pursue Me. Keep surrendering, become silent, sit in the solitude, fast, be in My Word, acknowledge Me in everything, be lonely, be disciplined, stay focused, and reflect on your dreams and the surroundings that I put before you. As you do, I will lead you to places you have not been or seen. I am taking you to your inner depths to reveal to you My truths. I am revealing to you what My Father promised. I am leading you to a high summit on a mountaintop. I want you to experience and see the supernatural gifts available to you. Your heart will feel overwhelmingly for creation and humanity, your ears will discern direction, your mind will increase in wisdom, your faith will have unlimited borders, and your soul will be at home and belong to Me in this foreign land. Finally, you will feel at home in your own skin and flesh, but new as who I created and intended you to be as a spiritual, loving, interconnected being. As you reach the ascended heights, you will share the gospel, love unconditionally, serve altruistically, inspire the brokenhearted, bring light to the hopeless, give voice to the poor, bring healing to the lost, and encourage all that you meet. Be prepared for Me to take you to center stage to be My spokesperson, clothed with My power and authority from on high. This is a mountaintop experience. Continue to follow Me.

Mark 12:30; Romans 6:11; 2 Corinthians 5:17; 1 John 2:6

November 30

Beautiful One,

Do not be misled or fall into the worldly trappings that say you must work harder in order to be successful. Success by worldly standards of arriving is temporal and only a false illusion. Success in God's economy is participating each day in your soul's life purpose and mission by giving freely and passionately of yourself to others, expecting nothing in return. You never arrive, but in this process, you become who I called and intended you to be: a good, faithful, humble, and loving servant to the least of these. And what you do to the least of these is what you do unto Me. There is no greater success than one who offers himself as a living sacrifice and fully surrenders to Me.

Daniel 12:2–3; Malachi 3:16–17 ;Romans 12:1–2

December 1

Beautiful One,

There will be storms and adversity that are going to come regardless of how much you abide in Me. In fact, attacks may become more frequent, with more ferocity and intensity. No matter what, do not give in or give up on the plans that I have for you. When a storm brews up unexpectedly, do not fight it, but just retreat and be still and quiet with assurance, knowing that this is My battle and not yours. Trust and believe in My outcome, patiently enduring until I reveal to you it is time to move forth. It is through the storms and adversity that I am increasing your faith and preparing you to become a leader to deliver hurt, broken, and lost souls. As painful a process as it all has been, the outcome is going to be a glorious and extraordinary unfolding that not even you could orchestrate in your own strength. Part of this preparation is to teach you how to humbly operate from My authority from on high. As the storm enfolds upon you to where you can't see anything, take refuge in My presence, not wavering in your faith. I know this will be scary, but do not look to other sources for your comfort or answers. It comes only from Me. Abide in Me. Will you trust Me in the middle of the roughest storm, knowing I am protecting you? Rebuke the storm, repeating that you trust and believe Me. Do not run from it, but stay with Me even in the worst storm. I am with you, and you still have My promises; there is nothing that has changed. Once the storm is over, you will realize you weren't harmed, but you were strengthened even more, giving you boldness, courage, and faith like you never before experienced. You just gained more quiet confidence and assurance in My Son, Jesus Christ. You will look back and realize that I brought you through the storm and that I will continue to do that for you no matter how fierce the storm may be. Continue to abide in Me in all circumstances.

Psalm 46:1; John 16:33; 2 Corinthians 10:15

December 2

Beautiful One,

This is a time to retreat with Me. I am calling you to be still and quiet with Me. Release your busyness and worldly distractions to spend a time of refuge and strengthening with Me. This is a necessary time so that I can refresh you and refill you with My love, joy, peace, and compassion because you have so freely been giving all of yourself to others. Take this time seriously to rest often in My presence so that I can rejuvenate you with even more capacity to go out and give for the next phase that I am preparing you for. Do not be distracted during this time with the enemy's deceitful lies of making you feel guilty or inadequate for not doing more with your free time. This is our special time where I want to pamper you with My love, letting you know how I see you. This is also a time of revealing more of how I am going to use you to serve humanity in My name. Come to Me and find rest, solace, peace, comfort, and joy during this time because you deserve it, but more importantly, I want to pour into you how much I cherish and love you, My child.

Matthew 14:23; Luke 11:1; James 4:8; Revelation 2:2–5

Beautiful One,

Stop comparing yourself and your journey with others. This is the enemy using anything to guide you into the pit of negative thinking and condemnation. Condemnation is not of Me. The enemy wants you to feel condemned and empty, like you are missing out on worldly relationships, pleasures, and desires. There is a fierce battle going on around you, making you feel this way. The enemy is trying to do everything in his power to separate you from God's will and love. Yes, I know it appears that others are having the time of their lives, but I am calling you to complete abandon and radical obedience. Don't settle for instant pleasure and gratification because that is mediocre living. Eve's sinful choice in Genesis in the Garden of Eden was followed by more generational sin, where her one son killed his brother. Jesus is your example during these times because He was tempted for forty days by Satan in the desert. Jesus' radical obedience turned the world upside down into a ministry that went against the ways of the world. Jesus said yes to My will in the Garden of Gethsemane, where we know the end of the story where Jesus triumphed over death. I too have an extraordinary outcome for you if you keep saying yes by walking in My radical obedience. Don't settle for less for instant gratification during your lonely moments. Come to Me to fill that need for you by drawing closer and nearer to Me.

John 21:15–23

December 4

Beautiful One,

Rest in Me. Release and let go of every thought, feeling, or desire that comes you way. The enemy is trying to distract you by creating confusion and spontaneous ambitions, strivings, and decisions. Retreat into My presence so that I can care for and protect you. I will give you peace and contentment during this phase so you don't make any irrational decisions that are not from Me. Come lay your head upon My lap, and I will alleviate all your fears and concerns. I am asking you to have obedient and courageous faith, which will diminish the doubts, fears, and mistrust you are experiencing. Rest and abide in Me. I have this, and the victory is mine. It is just another one of the enemy's tactics to distract you from the vision that I have placed upon your heart. Nothing is too great for Me to overcome. Rest, be still, and silent until this too has passed. You will then see why the enemy was working so diligently to frazzle you. You are nearly ready to walk into more of My abundance, and blessings are about to come your way.

Exodus 23:1–2; Proverbs 29:25; Philippians 4:8

Beautiful One,

Don't fall into the trappings of desiring the worldly ways of relationships, busyness, strivings, or adventure to fill your void or emptiness. These are all temporary and will never completely fill your emptiness, and you will continue to strive for more and more false illusions to fill your emptiness. Only solitude and silence with Me can fill you with an everlasting joy and a soul's life purpose that will never fade away. It is because you are in My presence where I am freely flowing My love in, through, and out of you. You become a new transformed person because My love is filling you in a way that nothing in this world can compare to. My love then gets radiated out from you into others, meeting them right where they are. This is the relationship, the adventure, and the work that I want you to do willingly. It's a focused time and rhythm of silence and solitude with Me every day. It is this type of productivity that will bring you success and abundance not of this world. You will be finely prepared to walk between the heavenly and earthly realm, serving and loving others, where My love will be infinite and unending. This is the adventure that I am calling you to: to live a life fully operating in My power and authority, free from bondage and strongholds, to one of freedom with an all-knowing, seeing, and loving soul to bring about healing and transformation to lost, broken souls. To the world, My seeing, My ways, and My wisdom seem foolish, but continue to increase your faith in Me, and I will reveal more to you about My economy and way of being that is available to you. Come and abide in Me in My presence in silence and solitude. It is a time to prosper to your full potential.

Proverbs 20:3; 1 Thessalonians 4:10–12; 1 Timothy 5:12–14

Beautiful One,

Just as Daniel refused the food and wine of the king's royal table, I too am calling you to refuse the food and wine of the world. This is anything that has become culturally and socially a norm that is toxic to your soul and well-being. What keeps you separated and distracted from Me? Seek My guidance for Me to reveal to you these worldly foods. Let your inner being be your guide. It could be certain impure and immoral relationships, social settings, the food you consume, the activities you engage in, political strife, economic injustices, or social structures that are not of Me. You are being called to resist and choose not to participate in the enemy's schemes of what has become the social norm. You have an example from My Son, Jesus, to reject these injustices and immoral behaviors that will lead to the eventual drying of your bones, hardening of your heart, and loss of control. You are jeopardizing the well-being of your heart, mind, body, and soul to the enemy. Do not waver in any of your choices that would separate you from My righteousness. The more you reject these temptations, the easier it becomes and the closer you get to Me, the center of My heart. The closer you get to Me, the more you gain My sight, My vision, My compassion, My hearing, My desires, and My ways. The closer you get to Me, the more you want to be with Me, desiring to feel and be at the center of My heart. Your choices and decisions will become so obvious that you will mourn the choices and decisions of others who continue to live in the flesh of temporary worldly desires. You are finally arriving at home at one with Me in your fleshly body, awakening to the peace that you can experience here on earth as it is in heaven. Once you get a taste of this, the more you will want that which not only strengthens you, but also gives you the authority and capacity to empower others to live this way. There is even more, Beautiful One. I will reveal it to you in the silence, in the solitude, and in your time of fasting. Stay so close to Me that you lose sight of everything else you see.

Daniel 1:8–16

December 7

Beautiful One,

Become light as a feather and flow effortlessly where I lead you. Do not resist the currents of the wind, but let My breath carry you. As you are freely floating, remain silent during this time. Be at peace and carefree, enjoying each thing that I put before you. Don't go seeking or striving to put things into motion in your own strength, but watch where I land you and how I answer your prayers. There is nothing you need to do on your own other than to be willing to free-fall, trusting that I have you, knowing you are in My protection. When you fully release and surrender to Me, you will gain inner strength with a graceful authority to compassionately serve and win over others on My behalf. In this newfound freedom, you are being empowered for great things ahead that are about to unfold. Float freely in My care, trusting Me.

Job 17:9; Proverbs 4:18; Ezekiel 36:27

December 8

Beautiful One,

Let go and just fall into My care and presence. If you grasp at wanting to know where I am going to take you, you still have not let go of control. Let go of your plans and desires, and fall freely like a feather. The more freely you float and fall, the more I am able to take you to the inner depths of My heart. This is the way of least resistance. It is at the center of My being that you can experience unhindered all that I have for you. You will be at one with Me, able to fully function with My wisdom, knowledge, and capabilities. This is a time to soar to greater heights. The quieter you become, the more peace you will have. The more you surrender, the greater the power and authority you will gain. The more you release your plans to Me, the more significant plans I can use you for. You see, your ways are obstacles and hinder what I have for you. Freely fall and float graciously so you can transcend to what I have for you. Your plans are good, but My plans are greater. Don't restrict your plans to just good because of your need to be in control. Let Me show you My glorious plans for you. I am at the center of your entire being. Don't be afraid of anything. Freely fall. I will not fail or forsake you. I am the wind beneath your wings, and it's a time to soar to greater heights. The way is opening up and becoming clear.

Isaiah 22:22; Micah 2:13; 2 Corinthians 2:12

December 9

Beautiful One,

This is a time for you and Me to draw in closer and nearer to each other. In this time of silence and solitude, I want you to be present with Me, fully focused only upon Me. Let go of all other distractions that you typically busy yourself with. This is a time for Me to cherish you by filling you with My radiant warmth, My pulsating touch, and a love that pierces you to the inner core of your soul. It is a time to rest in My loving arms, allowing Me to fill you with My impassioned love. Melt into My caress, where you become so free and light that you cherish and long for this to be the only place you want to be. I am touching those places within your soul that have been deeply wounded and violated. No longer will these deep wounds of hurt, pain, and despair control you. My love is a balm to these raw wounds that will now become healed scars symbolizing your strength, resiliency, and will to persevere, allowing nothing to hold you back. By My stripes, Beautiful One, your wounds have been healed. My anointing touch has released those chains, and you have been set free. Yes, claim and receive that in My name. You have been set free!

Psalm 107:14; 147:3; Isaiah 53:5

Beautiful One,

Take deep breaths while sitting in the silence of My presence. Let go of anxious feelings and thoughts while releasing them into My care. The enemy is trying to get you stirred up with these inferior feelings and emotions to distract you from being focused upon Me. Breathe in newness, trusting to let go and give up control so that I can reveal to you what is next. That is the tension of flesh and spirit you are anxiously feeling. The flesh is clinging, while the spirit wants to deliver new to you. There are some important sweeping changes taking place around you that you are not conscious of. I have heard your prayers and they are manifesting, but it has been an intense spiritual battle in order to get them to fruition. Continue to pray, be immersed in My Word, meditate in the silence, fast, seek, and praise Me in every detail of your life. Be steadfast and immovable in your convictions of My truth and promises. Trust and believe that I have already answered your prayers even though you can't see them yet. In all of this, you are protected, so do not waver, doubt, or worry about what others say or think concerning where I am leading and guiding you. These things that I am about to bring to pass are aligned with My divine plan and timing. It is all for a higher purpose and calling that I am about to propel you into. You are on the right path, so remain confident and joyful for what I am about to reveal to you. All of your gifts and skills will be used to minister to others in My name. Hallelujah!

Psalm 70:5; Nehemiah 6:9

Beautiful One,

There is no condemnation or judgment toward you when you come to Me in your weakness, confessing your sinful thoughts. I am encouraged and commend you for bringing it to Me, admitting that you know you can't fight this inner struggle on your own. I see your heart for wanting to do what is right and good, but sin is always lurking around you, deceiving your heart, mind, body, and soul. Because you are now in Christ Jesus, you have been set free from sin and death. The Spirit now lives inside of you and continues to groan toward union with Me, seeking My righteousness. It is a process that comes with suffering, but you do not suffer alone, for you are an heir to My glory. Your sufferings are temporary, so wait patiently and eagerly as I work on behalf of your weaknesses. The Holy Spirit is interceding for you and knows what you need during this time of inner struggle, strife, and desires. I am working all things out for those who love Me, whom I have called according to My purpose. There is nothing greater than Me that can come against you. Abide in Me, and draw closer and nearer to Me. Nothing can separate you from Me. I have chosen you, and I graciously give you all things that were destined before you were even born.

Romans 8

December 12

Beautiful One,

It is a time and season where I am taking you deeper, asking you to let go of more of your habitual patterns of behavior that no longer serve you. I am asking you to participate with Me in a greater capacity and a new way. It is a process of allowing Me to have complete control and will over your life. I need you to become like a tree that goes through the seasons of life that is planted firmly in fertile soil. I am that fertile soil so that your roots can grow deep within Me and My firm foundation. The deeper your roots, the more capable you are to sustain during unforeseen circumstances such as a drought, torrential rains, harsh winds, ice storms, or a snowy blizzard. All of this work of growing from an immature sapling sitting in the silence, being in solitude, fasting, praying, and meditating is taking you deeper. Your roots have to go deep within My Word, truths, and promises so that you will be unhindered by not only the temptations of sin around you, but also the influence of social and cultural norms in today's society. The significance of the work, the vision, and ministry that I have called you to requires a lot of preparation for a deeply rooted spiritually mature tree. It is a slow, steady process that can't be rushed, but one of steadfast care, nurturing, nourishment, and gentleness. By this divine order and preparation, you will be equipped to go out and soar to do what I have called you to fulfill, not weakened or blindsided by the harsh elements of the world.

Hosea 10:12; Ephesians 3:17; Colossians 2:7–8

Beautiful One,

I am calling you to a mountaintop experience again. It is a time for Me to nourish and fill you with My love and care. It is a gift to you during this season of where I have you. Do not get sidetracked or lose focus on Me because you are caught in what others are doing. That is why I have asked you to disconnect from the busyness of the world and social media so that you don't get caught up in the false illusions that others are portraying. I am the same yesterday, today, and tomorrow, and My plans for you have not changed. Have faith, and continue to trust and believe that a joyous season is coming your way soon. As significant as this vision is, that is how deep I have had to take you to prepare you for it. Your prayers are manifesting, but it is all in My preparation and timing. Simply obey and rest in Me.

Mark 13:33–37; Luke 12:35–38

Beautiful One,

I chose and anointed you before you were even conceived in your mother's womb. You were destined to do many great things for My honor and glory. You are beginning to understand the depth of your calling, and you are humbled and weep with honor and gratitude that I chose you. I too am honored and weep that you have obediently accepted this calling. Let go of more dreams, plans, and situations that are dead and not going anywhere. They no longer can serve you because you are not that same individual anymore. Do not fear or doubt the new plans that I have coming your way that are much better than what you had planned. I am going to use all of your talents and knowledge to serve others in positive and life-transforming ways. Your obedience and willingness to serve Me with all your heart, soul, and mind will bring about joyous blessings in your life. Continue to persevere and you will receive what I have promised.

Hebrews 10:19–27, 35–36

December 15

Beautiful One,

I give you free will to choose your path, but not many take seriously or heed the calling that I have placed upon their hearts because of their own selfish or worldly desires. You have allowed Me to gently and compassionately take control of your life, purging you of false personas and hidden sin, which I know has been very painful for you. No longer do fear, control, denial, pride, lust, desire, and doubt hold you in bondage. I have delivered you from these strongholds and set you free in the name of My Son, Jesus Christ. These very deeply rooted dark places within you have been exposed to My light, revealing and affirming your soul's life purpose and passion. Under all of the pressure and friction of refining you, you are becoming like a precious pearl in My eyes. You are beginning to see and understand your deeper soul purpose, where you are open to receive and claim it. With that, many well-deserved blessings of My prosperity and abundance are about to be showered upon you. Cling to Me and what is true. Persevere on this current path and do not let your heart be troubled, but trust in Me and only Me. Do not lose focus on what I have revealed to you. By remaining in Me, I will remain in you. Whatever you ask for in My name, it will be given to you. This is how I show My glory so that you may bear much fruit as My chosen and anointed disciple.

John 14:1–4, 12–14; 16:23–24

Beautiful One,

During our time of silence, I was prompting you to look at a painful truth that you continue to deny. It has been a hindrance and obstacle for Me to take you to the next spiritual realm of where you can experience union with Me. You became angry and indignant, but you noticed that I stayed with you right where you were. I already knew this was going to be your response, and I affirmed you for voicing it and bringing it to Me. This brought it to light, which allowed Me to lovingly and compassionately reveal to you not only the depth of sin, but also the consequences of sin. Sin runs deep, and I know you were born into this sinful world with generational curses already upon you before you ever spoke a word. It is important to understand the context of your family, history, circumstances, and own narrative in relation to the social context. However, I caution you that it does not give you permission to continue to sin because of My known grace. You are no longer spiritually immature or ignorant of My Word. You know My Word, truth, and promises, and this invites you to pursue My ways of righteousness in order to become formed in My image. I know your flesh is weak, so you can't do it alone. That is why you must abide in Me and My Word faithfully. My Word is your defense and sword against the enemy's attacks of deceit, lies, and rationale. My Word must be impressed upon your heart, mind, and body so that you are equipped for this spiritual battle. Everyday society and cultural norms are changing and becoming tolerant of sin, but I say to you, My word is unchanging. I am the same yesterday, today, and tomorrow. So I encourage you to pursue righteousness, godliness, love, endurance and gentleness.

1 Timothy 5:24–25; 6:11

Beautiful One,

I love to surprise My chosen and called one. As you have wrestled with this calling upon your life with excuses of not being wise, intelligent, or able to articulate things well, it is the very reason I chose you. I choose and use the foolish and the most unlikely individuals because in their weakness and fears, My strength and wisdom are made known to the rest of the foolish world. I will give you wisdom and strength that come from the authority of the cross, which bears My almighty power. I know where you have been and what you have done, but more importantly, I know what you are being equipped to do on My behalf for the glory of My kingdom. You know the depth of My love, grace, and mercy, which humbles you not to boast about your works and deeds, but to boast about My work in you that is also promised for all My children. My wisdom has been hidden within you for such a time as this that I destined long ago. No eye has seen, no ear has heard, no mind has conceived what I have prepared for those who love Me, but I have revealed it to you by My Spirit and not by the spirit of the world. The spirit of the world perishes, but My Spirit is eternal truths and promises. As you are in Me and I in you, you have the mind of Christ, who is work in you and endures forever.

1 Corinthians 1:18–31; 2:1–16

Beautiful One,

Even though you have suffered greatly and made many sacrifices, it all is not in vain. It is all for My glory as you will see when I reveal it to you. My great works in you will be revealed soon, so continue to exalt My name through the pain, suffering, trials, and joy. I am making all things new and possible. Do not be afraid of the changes, the trials, the challenges, or the vision that I have placed upon your heart. As you continue to walk obediently with Me, I will guide you each and every step, opening the way to places you never conceived of having opportunities for. I have given you new life and an inheritance that will never perish, spoil, or fade that is in heaven for you by your faith that is shielded by My power. In all of this, rejoice, even though you suffer grief in all kinds of trials. These sufferings have come so that your faith may be extended, refined, and proven genuine. Therefore, prepare your mind for action, be self-controlled, and set your hope fully on the grace to be given you. As an obedient child, do not conform to evil desires you had when you lived in ignorance. Be holy in all you do. Be holy because I am holy. If you suffer because of what is right, you are blessed.

1 Peter 1:4–15

Beautiful One,

In the depths of your inner being and subconscious, you have experienced My greatest gift to you. I have taken you to the inner depths of your subconscious, which resembles a dark, smelly, damp, and cold crawl space. By your openness and allowing Me to continue to take you to those places, slowly but steadily, hidden sin, inferior thoughts, and past decay have been revealed to you. Each time you acknowledge one of these places, it brings more of My light to this place, making it easier to go deeper. My light in these places also releases the strongholds and bondages that have been in your life. Now I can reveal to you more of your gifts and creativity because this blocking obstacle is removed. You are now becoming lighter, freer, and purer, clearing more of the way to receive and work in My power and authority. This weed pulling that you have been doing in your subconscious of these painful parts of yourself is no longer as difficult to face because I have showered you with rain for this process at this time. Just as the rain makes the ground soft, making it easier to pull weeds, My rainwater has softened your defenses and made you open to go to these difficult places. My rainwater has flooded your subconscious, allowing you to do the necessary work. You just realized that My rainwater is the gift, the ultimate gift that anyone can receive. Yes, this gift is always there and available for you even when you don't realize it, but you are embodying, living, and abiding in this gift now. When you get to this place of embodying, living, and abiding in this gift, you are walking in step with Me and the way that I want you to go. This gift can't be rationalized, and only until you experience the depth of it do you realize that I have now equipped you with this gift for your work with others. In the gift of My rain, it has been revealed to you that it is My gift of grace. You just experienced My sanctifying *grace*.

Psalm 103

367

Beautiful One,

I have called you to be fruitful, to increase and multiply on the earth, and to increase upon it. This is not for your selfish gain, but to work purposefully at finding your way and soul's life mission for here on earth. You are to serve all of humanity and My creation. This means for you to work wholeheartedly as if you are doing everything for Me. Everything that you do reflects back to Me, others, and My creation. We are all interdependent and interconnected. Everything that you do affects the system and order of the entire universe. In everything you do, be self-controlled, gentle, kind, patient, loving, and obedient so that harmony and unity can be experienced here on earth as I intended. This is the peace that I intended for here on earth as it is in heaven. I am your God, the one and only God. As I have instructed you before, love Me with all your heart, soul, mind, body, and strength, and love your neighbors as yourself. This also includes all of My creation. Everything you do reflects back your love for Me and My creation. It is a sign of your reverence, love, and honor for Me.

Genesis 1:28; 9:7; 22:17

Beautiful One,

You are realizing that you are now living, embodying, and abiding in My grace. This is a place of deep humility and gratitude. I see your tears of humbleness and joy. I hear your thoughts of your unworthiness to receive My grace. This is a place that I will be able to use you, fully equipping you with My power and authority for the next tasks at hand that I have for you. Continue to bask in My presence in the silence and solitude. Continue to seek Me in every detail of your life, praising Me for each and every minor detail. This pleases Me, seeing you fully open and abiding in My grace. I want you free to experience all that I have for you. No longer will past sin or inferior thoughts weigh you down and hold you back. You are walking into the next spiritual phase that I have for you. It is a time to now flourish, to go out and unfold this ministry while I continue to increase your development. I know your suffering has been long, but a joyous harvest and unfolding are about to come forth just as I promised you when we began this journey together.

Romans 5:1–11; Ephesians 2:8–9

December 22

Beautiful One,

My grace abounds in you. No longer does sin control you or selfish desires lead you, but My sanctifying grace covers, abides, and surrounds you. It is a gift I freely give that you have received, which turns you away from evil desires. My grace that you have embodied has created a deeper loyalty and commitment within your core. My grace is at times overwhelming, where you experience sincere adoration and reverence for Me. My grace is a visceral feeling that warmly radiates through your entire being, empowering you with a humbled passion. Now take My gift of grace that you have received and share it with others. Live into My sufficient grace in every detail of your life through your words, deeds, actions, work, and service. My abiding grace is leading, guiding, and protecting you as you serve My kingdom. Be aware of My presence in all things, acknowledging and boasting that this is My work alone. I am holding your life and destiny in the palm of My hands.

Romans 5:3–4; 6:14–15

December 23

Beautiful One,

You are right where you are supposed to be. Stop trying to navigate yourself into other places. I need you right here, right now so that you can continue to be an example to others who need to see your positive influence and My light. Many are watching you. You don't see it or realize it, but you are transforming and affirming others' lives. Be patient and endure this phase where I have you. Trust and believe in Me and My divine timing. It is all going to work out and be okay. Just wait and you will see. Keep doing each thing that I put before you. I am with you and taking you to new places and heights that you never would have imagined. Just relax in this place by becoming as light as a feather, allowing Me to gently shift you toward the path that I have set for you. Allow yourself to experience My works, grace, and witness as pure joy. Even though this has been an enduring process, I hope you feel the joyous deeds that I am accomplishing through you. Grace, peace, and protection abound in you for this journey.

Matthew 19:26, 29; 20:26; 21:21

Beautiful One,

You are My precious child in whom I delight. I have seen your devoted heart and faith to Me in all of your circumstances. You continue to press in and forward through all the trials and adversity that have been before you. You have shown a steadfast love and commitment to the work that I am doing within you. Be assured that your labor has not been done in vain. Continue to be strong, and do not give up, for you and your work will be rewarded. I will bless you by enlarging your territory. My hand is upon you, protecting you from any harm or pain. I will surely continue to be with you, leading you in the way that you should go. I have called you to righteousness, where I will keep you so that you can be a vessel to help open the eyes of the blind, to help set the captives free from prison, and to release those who are sitting in the darkness. See, I am at work in and through you, doing a new thing. There is a burst of passion and energy within you that is springing forth, but you don't fully perceive it. You are on a lonely path that is narrow and less traveled, but My mysterious works and deeds that I reveal to you inspire you to endure and persevere no matter what comes your way. Do not lose heart. I am training you for a marathon so that you will be equipped for spiritual battle and the deliverance of My people, whom I love greatly. I know what is best for you and the greater good of My people. I am directing all your steps. Run the good race that I have called you to by trusting Me with unwavering faith.

Isaiah 42:6–7; 43:19; 48:17 ; 2 Chronicles 15:7

December 25

Beautiful One,

Your devoted loyalty, faith, and trust in Me have provided you with spiritual light and contentment that you are right where you are supposed to be. This "knowing" has created a peace within you that has dissipated your clinging habits and fearful thoughts. Continue to trust in My divine timing as I orchestrate a breakthrough so that your desire and prayers will be manifested. Remain still, patient, and wait upon Me with an open heart so that I can lead you in the way you should go without hesitation. Abandon your previous way of striving to perform and to be needed. Allow Me to transform this maladaptive way into one that I will channel into a focused divine energy and passion to serve altruistically that is life-giving not only to you, but also for the greatest good of humanity. I am equipping you with charity that is in line with your calling for your work and ministry. The closer and more intimate you are with Me, the more invigorated and passionate you are for the work that I have called you to. I am freeing you from spiritual poverty, delivering you from strongholds, and liberating you to experience life with harmony, joy, peace, and love. From out of your spiritually immature past, I am bringing the things in your unconsciousness to consciousness, equipping you with My wisdom and knowledge. From this place, you can speak and sit with others no matter where they are on their journeys. It is My grace that has brought you here at this divine timing. Sit in the silence in My presence, listening for My whispers of the next steps. Don't go before Me. Wait for Me patiently.

Romans 5 and 8

Beautiful One,

As you sit more with Me in My presence in the silence, I will give you more glimpses of My vision and ministry. I see your heart, passion, and the energy that is bursting forth within you that feels hard to contain. I will continue to give you only nuggets of affirmation, leading to the unfolding of this vision through people that I put into your life, through words spoken to you, and through My whispers of revelation of your next steps. Your obedience of fasting, silence, and solitude has allowed you to grow and experience Me in a new spiritual realm. I know at times you feel distant from Me, but I am closer to you than I have ever been before. I am asking you to trust this phase with a spiritual knowing that I am orchestrating and manifesting answered prayers even though you can't presently see it. You can't see or comprehend all of My glorious and mysterious works, but I am with you with bursting, impassioned energy. There is a breakthrough that is about to propel you into the next spiritual realm. I know this makes you uncomfortable with fear because none of this was in your plans, so I command you to be strong and very courageous. Be careful to obey Me in all ways. Do not turn from it to the right or to the left, that you may be successful wherever you go. In order to move you along into the next spiritual realm, I need to take you out of your comfort zone. I don't want you to become too content where you are because you then become stagnant and mediocre, and then you will tend to fall back into your primitive habits of operating in your own strength and not mine. I want to shower you with My abundant and overflowing grace so that those watching you will see My glorious works through you. Keep coming, and keep saying yes. This is where your faithful steps will meet My grace that is exceedingly sufficient to do more than you even thought possible. Where faith and grace meet on earth, there is a supernatural power and authority from heaven that empowers others to be transformed.

Joshua 1:7

December 27

Beautiful One,

You are beginning to experience more of My freedom, realizing that there is nothing that you have to do other than to follow and obey Me. Do not compromise the vision and ministry that I have revealed to you for your personal desires. The enemy is prowling and trying to deceive you into settling for instant gratification. It is not possible to progress when you are clinging to false desires while also wanting to walk in My authority to carry out the ministry that I have laid upon your heart. It does not work that way. There is no negotiating between the two because I have already ordained this for you before you were even conceived in your mother's womb. My plans and ways do not change, nor do My purposes and plans for your life. Stay focused upon Me and the vision that I have given you. I am shifting you into another spiritual realm if you will release even more of yourself to Me so that I can liberate you. Do not be distracted by the worldly noise. Through Me, you will achieve the impossible.

1 Peter 1:3–9

Beautiful One,

You have a sincere gift of faith, and it is your faith that has healed you. I have seen your dedication to Me through your prayer life where you have spiritually matured. As you continue to dedicate more of yourself to Me by drawing in closer to Me, you are becoming one and at home in becoming true to yourself. This is the longing and desire that you have yearned for. It is a feeling of holiness, purity, and a clear conscience. Stay on this journey, longing to be even closer to Me so that nothing will distract you or lead you astray from this personal conviction. You are becoming steadfast, unshakable, and immovable. It is all because of your dependence upon Me and your faith that has healed you. During this phase, you will not completely understand what is happening, but stay where you are for the moment, doing each thing that I put before you. You are being used as a witness to others through your righteous acts, deeds, service, and words. Endure this part of the journey, finding the joy and pleasure in it. I promise you, it will be worth it, and you will see a joyous harvest from your love, faith, and obedience to Me. Keep doing each absurd thing that surfaces, and watch how I reveal and give you the most impossible. It will be glorious.

Luke 4:18–19

December 29

Beautiful One,

Do not worry about the details of the day. I have already taken care of them for you. Today you should go about your appointments and obligations as though you were meeting with Me. Each person you will be serving, meeting, or sending correspondence via e-mail should be as though you were working for Me. Each interaction you have with others is an opportunity to disciple them, allowing them to see Me through you. Be present with each individual, not worrying about the next task and deadlines. I have those details that often distract you from ministering to the ones that I put before you. Don't worry about time. Allow yourself to listen deeply, to minister and encourage a loving relationship without hurry and haste. What the individuals need whom I put before you is your time, feeling heard and as though they are the most important person to you. It should be just like it is when I am with you, and how I treat you with patience, love, kindness, and gentleness. You are My hands, feet, words, and deeds. Let others see and experience Me through you in all that you do. Ask Me to lead, guide, and show you how to be excellent without personal preconceived plans, desires, or agendas. Just be. Everything else will fall into its proper place.

Luke 10:39–41; 12:22–34

Beautiful One,

As I continue to peel back the layers of hidden sin, inferior thoughts, and defenses, I am also strengthening your inner core to where you are becoming who I intended you to be. This process has been humbling to you, but you have been able to experience My all-sufficient, invincible grace. As you open yourself more, allowing Me into these painful places, I will transform it into more of your innate gifts and creativity that will be used in the ministry for My glory and not for your personal gain. In fact, the more you receive My grace, the more you want to give this gift away because it is too powerful and exhilarating to hold on to. You want others to be empowered and inspired by this gift. Your ability to be able to receive My gift of grace with detachment, where it flows in, through, and out of you to others, makes it possible for Me to freely flow through as an empty vessel because I know you won't attach to it as an addiction or idol, abusing the gift and power. The more you give away, the more I can trust you with more of My gifts to be received so that you can use and give them to others in a life-giving and altruistic way. I am making you stronger, equipping you for the journey ahead. Remain focused with your eyes only upon Me. I will continue to do glorious works in and through you. Trust and believe.

Isaiah 30:15, 19–26

Beautiful One,

You have questioned and asked so often, "What is the purpose in all of my pain and suffering?" I assure you that it has a deeper meaning that goes beyond you. It is becoming clear to you that as I have been present with you in your pain and suffering, I have been surfacing things within your inner depths that need to be acknowledged, such as your sins, inferior thoughts, and negative attitudes. It has been a time of refining and purging you. It has been a time of testing and increasing your faith beyond your borders and comfort zone. I had to know if you were truly devoted to Me and trusted Me with all your heart, mind, body, and soul. I needed reassurance that you were ready and equipped for the calling and vision that I have placed upon you. If you were able to withstand the fires and the overflowing waters where I led you, while still praising Me, I knew that I could entrust you with this vision. I promise you, as you continue to walk in step with Me, I will take care of everything for you, enabling you to do amazing things in My name. Your suffering was also a time of humbling you so that you would not become boastful with pride. It was a time to conform you to the image and likeness of My Son, Jesus Christ. What I am calling you to, I am asking you to be My ambassador, a living example of serving, loving, and meeting the needs of others. Your pain has not been for nothing. This is greater than you. Praise Me and sing hallelujah for My choosing you. Watch what I do.

Ephesians 4:2; 1 Peter 3:3–4

January 1

Beautiful One,

The time is near when a major breakthrough is about to happen. Another phase in your life is ending so that the new creative gifts within you can emerge. You have been under intense strongholds and bondages that have been holding you back. The internal vibrations that you have experienced have been My love and grace gently shifting and exposing this dragon within you. No longer does this dragon have control over you, and now you can continue to transform to the next level where I am taking you. The creative gift that has been released is that of humility and humbleness. It is from this place that I can use you to authentically serve Me and others that I put before you. No longer does the dragon of ulterior motives, manipulative ways, or selfish gain control you. This has been an intense battle of spiritual warfare where I have delivered you from this stronghold. You are one step closer to realizing the vision that I have placed upon you so that you can help to transform many lives for so much good. This is a significant breakthrough, and that is why you have experienced so much resistance and conflict. Continue to trust and believe Me.

Proverbs 4:25–27; Ephesians 1:3; 6:18

January 2

Beautiful One,

I have equipped you with My strength, boldness, and courage to continue on this path that I have ordained for you. I have angels of protection around you so that you can continue to walk in the way that I am leading and directing you. There will be worldly distractions that will try to interfere with where you know I am calling you. Take heart—My plans have not changed. You have been anointed and have the authority to rebuke the enemy's tactics so that you do not waver or compromise everything that I have done for you. Bring your whole self and tithings to Me, and you will see Me throw open the floodgates of heaven and pour out so much blessing that you will not have room enough for it. I will prevent pests from devouring your crops, and the vines in your fields will not cast their fruit. All nations will call you blessed, for yours will be a delightful land. For you who revere My name, the sun of righteousness will rise with healing in its wings. You will trample down the wicked; they will be ashes under your feet. In this new year, stay devoted to Me with obedience, humility, truth, purity, and love, and you will meet your destiny with success that I planned long ago.

Deuteronomy 8:7–18; Psalm 92; Malachi 3:6–18; 4:1–3

Beautiful One,

Continue to say yes and persevere on the path where I have you. You have come upon the bottleneck part of the narrow path. This is why you are experiencing a period of feeling intense friction and disorientation. Once you get through this tight and narrow passage, the way will open up. This can be the most intense part of the journey, which is similar to giving birth. Just as the baby is about to push forth from the mother's womb, there is intense pain, pressure, and pushing that must happen. Keep pushing through the pain and discomfort that you are experiencing. As the baby is pushed into the physical world, all of the pain and discomfort is filled with joy and enthusiasm. That is what you will experience once you push through this narrow passage. You will experience joy, passion, and your destiny for what I have intended for you. Press in and press on, persevering with courage on the path that is before you with hope and expectancy. This is the year of new birth!

Psalm 18:30; 2 Corinthians 1:20; James 4:8

Beautiful One,

You were thirsty, I gave you living water.
You were broken, I met your every need.
You labored for righteousness, I satisfied your longing soul.
You were looking for someone to trust, I made an everlasting covenant for you.
You have an impassioned vision, I have endowed you with splendor.
You sought Me out, I came nearer.
You fought the enemy attacks, I had mercy upon you.
You humbled yourself before Me, I revealed My higher ways and thoughts.
You were empty, I filled and nourished you.
You received My love, I yielded many seeds within you.
You had no words, I imparted to you grace-filled messages.
You wanted more, I provided you with purpose.
You were in despair, I filled you with joy.
You were unsettled, I led you to peace.
You surrendered all, I am orchestrating to restore abundantly.
You wait upon Me, I promise "you" will never be destroyed! Amen.

(Inspired and adapted from Isaiah 55)

Beautiful One,

You are gaining vision for the things not of this physical world. Keep your eyes on the *vision*, resting in My promises and blessed assurance. Look toward My higher ways and thoughts. Be obedient and seek My holiness. My Spirit surrounds you, protecting you from the enemy and your foes. The closer you come into My presence, the more you will experience My glory. As you decrease, My kingdom within you increases, enlarging your capacity for what is yet to come. The more that I dwell within you, there is no room for anything unholy. Stay focused, persevere, keep near, and don't give up. You are on the narrow path where I am leading you to your destiny. You are *free*—free to be and to move about wherever I call you to go. There is nothing that can hold you back now Amen.

Psalm 23:4; Philippians 4:13; 1 Timothy 1:7

About The Author

Labawn holds a dual degree in Master of Arts in Counseling and Master of Divinity. LaDawn is compassionate about the well-being of others and advocates for social change in the community. Previously she volunteered her counseling services at a shelter for abused women and their kids who may be experiencing trauma and/or crisis situations. As part of her internship, she was a counselor in training at Family Life Resource Center in Harrisonburg. LaDawn served as Chaplain and Counselor at a male group home of formerly incarcerated felons preparing them for re-entry back into society. She also served as Chaplain at a local hospital. Currently LaDawn is principal broker/owner of Hometown Realty Group that is a God-led vision donating 100 percent of the company's annual net profits to a nonprofit that she founded, Hometown Rescue Mission and Ministry. The Rescue Mission once built will be a full time residence for the homeless, those with addictions and formerly incarcerated felons by providing a faith community of belonging. Weekly, LaDawn reserves 16 hours of pastoral counseling services to those who may not have health insurance or limited resources on a sliding fee income scale. LaDawn's first love and passion is being a mother to her daughter, Kendall. She enjoys spending as much time with her daughter as possible. She loves to write, create mosaic mandalas, garden, sports, golf, hiking, traveling, reading and constantly learning by immersing herself in diverse cultural experiences.

CPSIA information can be obtained
at www.ICGtesting.com
Printed in the USA
FSOW02n1847100317
31730FS